Financial Integration,
Corporate Governance,
and the Performance
of Multinational
Companies

Integrating National Economies: Promise and Pitfalls

Barry Bosworth (Brookings Institution) and Gur Ofer (Hebrew University)
Reforming Planned Economies in an Integrating World Economy

Ralph C. Bryant (Brookings Institution)
International Coordination of National Stabilization Policies

Susan M. Collins (Brookings Institution/Georgetown University)
Distributive Issues: A Constraint on Global Integration

Richard N. Cooper (Harvard University)
Environment and Resource Policies for the World Economy

Ronald G. Ehrenberg (Cornell University)
Labor Markets and Integrating National Economies

Barry Eichengreen (University of California, Berkeley)
International Monetary Arrangements for the 21st Century

Mitsuhiro Fukao (Bank of Japan)
Financial Integration, Corporate Governance, and the Performance of Multinational Companies

Stephan Haggard (University of California, San Diego)
Developing Nations and the Politics of Global Integration

Richard J. Herring (University of Pennsylvania) and Robert E. Litan (Department of Justice/Brookings Institution)
Financial Regulation in the Global Economy

Miles Kahler (University of California, San Diego)
International Institutions and the Political Economy of Integration

Anne O. Krueger (Stanford University)
Trade Policies and Developing Nations

Robert Z. Lawrence (Harvard University)
Regionalism, Multilateralism, and Deeper Integration

Sylvia Ostry (University of Toronto) and Richard R. Nelson (Columbia University)
Techno-Nationalism and Techno-Globalism: Conflict and Cooperation

Robert L. Paarlberg (Wellesley College/Harvard University)
Leadership Abroad Begins at Home: U.S. Foreign Economic Policy after the Cold War

Peter Rutland (Wesleyan University)
Russia, Eurasia, and the Global Economy

F. M. Scherer (Harvard University)
Competition Policies for an Integrated World Economy

Susan L. Shirk (University of California, San Diego)
How China Opened Its Door: The Political Success of the PRC's Foreign Trade and Investment Reforms

Alan O. Sykes (University of Chicago)
Product Standards for Internationally Integrated Goods Markets

Akihiko Tanaka (Institute of Oriental Culture, University of Tokyo)
The Politics of Deeper Integration: National Attitudes and Policies in Japan

Vito Tanzi (International Monetary Fund)
Taxation in an Integrating World

William Wallace (St. Antony's College, Oxford University)
Regional Integration: The West European Experience

Mitsuhiro Fukao

Financial Integration, Corporate Governance, and the Performance of Multinational Companies

THE BROOKINGS INSTITUTION
Washington, D.C.

Library of Congress Cataloging-in-Publication data:
Fukao, Mitsuhiro.
Financial integration, corporate governance, and the performance of
multinational companies/
Mitsuhiro Fukao
p.   cm.—(Integrating national economies, promise and pitfalls)
Includes bibliographical references and index.
ISBN 0-8157-2988-X (alk. paper : cloth)
ISBN 0-8157-2987-1 (alk. paper : pbk.)
1. International business enterprises—Finance—Management.
2. Corporate Governance. I. Title. II. Series: Integrating
national economies.
HG4027.5.F85   1995
658.15'99—dc20   94-46411
                                                        CIP

9 8 7 6 5 4 3 2 1

The paper used in this publication meets the minimum requirements of
American National Standard for Information Sciences—Permanence of Paper
for Printed Library Materials, ANSI Z39.48-1984

Typeset in Plantin

Composition by Princeton Editorial Associates
Princeton, New Jersey

Printed by R. R. Donnelley and Sons Co.
Harrisonburg, Virginia

Foreword

CORPORATIONS are organized differently from country to country in terms of their administrative structures, extent of shareholder power, and nature of corporate control. For the past decade, at least, policymakers, corporate managers, institutional investors, and scholars have debated the differences among structures and the implications for corporate competitiveness.

In this study, Mitsuhiro Fukao compares the structures of corporate governance in France, Germany, Japan, the United Kingdom, and the United States. He shows, for example, how differences in structure lead to stronger shareholder participation in German and Japanese companies, as well as more stable management and corporate relations with creditors, suppliers, and employees than are common in the United States and the United Kingdom. Meanwhile, in the United States and the United Kingdom, the stock markets have provided the means of corporate control, management turnover is higher, and employee relations more fluid. These basic differences have implications for the way business is or can be conducted. Stability often means lower capital costs and greater competitiveness, but it can also hinder companies from responding rapidly to new technology or from easily redeploying workers from declining sectors to growing ones, as is done more readily in the United States.

In the global context, financial markets have created strong pressures for more uniform rules on insider trading, takeover, and accounting and disclosure practices. Fukao encourages policymakers to assist and accelerate this convergence. But he does not support a single model of corporate governance because each system has its advantages and deeply rooted institutions.

When he began this project, Mitsuhiro Fukao was a senior economist for the Organization for Economic Cooperation and Development. He is now senior economist and division head of the Research and Statistics Department of the Bank of Japan. He was assisted in the course of the project by economists and officials of the Brookings Institution, the OECD, and the Bank of Japan. The author is especially grateful for valuable comments and suggestions on the manuscript from Margaret M. Blair, Ralph Bryant, Hideki Kanda, Hiroyuki Kansaku, Robert Z. Lawrence, Colin Mayer, Michael Porter, Stephen Prowse, Jay S. Siegel, Peter Strum, Motoaki Tazawa, and participants to preparatory conferences held at the Brookings Institution. The author also thanks Yasuko Morita for research assistance. Jim Schneider edited the manuscript, Laura Kelly verified its factual content, Lisa Guillory provided word processing, and Princeton Editorial Associates compiled the index.

Funding for the project came from the Center for Global Partnership of the Japan Foundation, the Curry Foundation, the Ford Foundation, the Korea Foundation, the Tokyo Club Foundation for Global Studies, the United States–Japan Foundation, and the Alex C. Walker Educational and Charitable Foundation. The author and Brookings are grateful for their support.

The views expressed here are those of the author and should not be ascribed to the people or organizations whose assistance is acknowledged above or to the trustees, officers, or staff members of the Brookings Institution.

BRUCE K. MACLAURY
President

March 1995
Washington, D.C.

Contents

Tables

Figures

Preface to the Studies on Integrating National Economies

E CONOMIC interdependence among nations has increased sharply in the past half century. For example, while the value of total production of industrial countries increased at a rate of about 9 percent a year on average between 1964 and 1992, the value of the exports of those nations grew at an average rate of 12 percent, and lending and borrowing across national borders through banks surged upward even more rapidly at 23 percent a year. This international economic interdependence has contributed to significantly improved standards of living for most countries. Continuing international economic integration holds out the promise of further benefits. Yet the increasing sensitivity of national economies to events and policies originating abroad creates dilemmas and pitfalls if national policies and international cooperation are poorly managed.

The Brookings Project on Integrating National Economies, of which this study is a component, focuses on the interplay between two fundamental facts about the world at the end of the twentieth century. First, the world will continue for the foreseeable future to be organized politically into nation-states with sovereign governments. Second, increasing economic integration among nations will continue to erode differences among national economies and undermine the autonomy of national governments. The project explores the opportunities and tensions arising from these two facts.

Scholars from a variety of disciplines have produced twenty-one studies for the first phase of the project. Each study examines the heightened competition between national political sovereignty and increased cross-border economic integration. This preface identifies background themes and issues common to all the studies and provides a brief overview of the project as a whole.[1]

Increasing World Economic Integration

Two underlying sets of causes have led nations to become more closely intertwined. First, technological, social, and cultural changes have sharply reduced the effective economic distances among nations. Second, many of the government policies that traditionally inhibited cross-border transactions have been relaxed or even dismantled.

The same improvements in transportation and communications technology that make it much easier and cheaper for companies in New York to ship goods to California, for residents of Strasbourg to visit relatives in Marseilles, and for investors in Hokkaido to buy and sell shares on the Tokyo Stock Exchange facilitate trade, migration, and capital movements spanning nations and continents. The sharply reduced costs of moving goods, money, people, and information underlie the profound economic truth that technology has made the world markedly smaller.

New communications technology has been especially significant for financial activity. Computers, switching devices, and telecommunications satellites have slashed the cost of transmitting information internationally, of confirming transactions, and of paying for transactions. In the 1950s, for example, foreign exchange could be bought and sold only during conventional business hours in the initiating party's time zone. Such transactions can now be carried out instantaneously twenty-four hours a day. Large banks pass the management of their worldwide foreign-exchange positions around the globe from one branch to another, staying continuously ahead of the setting sun.

Such technological innovations have increased the knowledge of potentially profitable international exchanges and of economic op-

---

1. A complete list of authors and study titles is included at the beginning of this volume, facing the title page.

portunities abroad. Those developments, in turn, have changed consumers' and producers' tastes. Foreign goods, foreign vacations, foreign financial investments—virtually anything from other nations—have lost some of their exotic character.

Although technological change permits increased contact among nations, it would not have produced such dramatic effects if it had been countermanded by government policies. Governments have traditionally taxed goods moving in international trade, directly restricted imports and subsidized exports, and tried to limit international capital movements. Those policies erected "separation fences" at the borders of nations. From the perspective of private sector agents, separation fences imposed extra costs on cross-bordertransactions. They reduced trade and, in some cases, eliminated it. During the 1930s governments used such policies with particular zeal, a practice now believed to have deepened and lengthened the Great Depression.

After World War II, most national governments began—sometimes unilaterally, more often collaboratively—to lower their separation fences, to make them more permeable, or sometimes even to tear down parts of them. The multilateral negotiations under the auspices of the General Agreement on Trade and Tariffs (GATT)—for example, the Kennedy Round in the 1960s, the Tokyo Round in the 1970s, and most recently the protracted negotiations of the Uruguay Round, formally signed only in April 1994—stand out as the most prominent examples of fence lowering for trade in goods. Though contentious and marked by many compromises, the GATT negotiations are responsible for sharp reductions in at-the-border restrictions on trade in goods and services. After the mid-1980s a large number of developing countries moved unilaterally to reduce border barriers and to pursue outwardly oriented policies.

The lowering of fences for financial transactions began later and was less dramatic. Nonetheless, by the 1990s government restrictions on capital flows, especially among the industrial countries, were much less important and widespread than at the end of World War II and in the 1950s.

By shrinking the economic distances among nations, changes in technology would have progressively integrated the world economy even in the absence of reductions in governments' separation fences. Reductions in separation fences would have enhanced interdependence even without the technological innovations. Together, these two sets of evolutionary changes have reinforced each other and strikingly transformed the world economy.

Changes in the Government of Nations

Simultaneously with the transformation of the global economy, major changes have occurred in the world's political structure. First, the number of governmental decisionmaking units in the world has expanded markedly, and political power has been diffused more broadly among them. Rising nationalism and, in some areas, heightened ethnic tensions have accompanied that increasing political pluralism.

The history of membership in international organizations documents the sharp growth in the number of independent states. For example, only 44 nations participated in the Bretton Woods conference of July 1944, which gave birth to the International Monetary Fund. But by the end of 1970, the IMF had 118 member nations. The number of members grew to 150 by the mid-1980s and to 178 by December 1993. Much of this growth reflects the collapse of colonial empires. Although many nations today are small and carry little individual weight in the global economy, their combined influence is considerable, and their interests cannot be ignored as easily as they were in the past.

A second political trend, less visible but equally important, has been the gradual loss of the political and economic hegemony of the United States. Immediately after World War II, the United States by itself accounted for more than one-third of world production. By the early 1990s the U.S. share had fallen to about one-fifth. Concurrently, the political and economic influence of the European colonial powers continued to wane, and the economic significance of nations outside Europe and North America, such as Japan, Korea, Indonesia, China, Brazil, and Mexico, increased. A world in which economic power and influence are widely diffused has displaced a world in which one or a few nations effectively dominated international decision-making.

Turmoil and the prospect of fundamental change in the formerly centrally planned economies compose a third factor causing radical changes in world politics. During the era of central planning, governments in those nations tried to limit external influences on their economies. Now leaders in the formerly planned economies are trying to adopt reforms modeled on Western capitalist principles. To the extent that these efforts succeed, those nations will increase their economic involvement with the rest of the world. Political and economic alignments among the Western industrialized nations will be forced to adapt.

Governments and scholars have begun to assess these three trends, but their far-reaching ramifications will not be clear for decades.

Dilemmas for National Policies

Cross-border economic integration and national political sovereignty have increasingly come into conflict, leading to a growing mismatch between the economic and political structures of the world. The effective domains of economic markets have come to coincide less and less with national governmental jurisdictions.

When the separation fences at nations' borders were high, governments and citizens could sharply distinguish "international" from "domestic" policies. International policies dealt with at-the-border barriers, such as tariffs and quotas, or responded to events occurring abroad. In contrast, domestic policies were concerned with everything behind the nation's borders, such as competition and antitrust rules, corporate governance, product standards, worker safety, regulation and supervision of financial institutions, environmental protection, tax codes, and the government's budget. Domestic policies were regarded as matters about which nations were sovereign, to be determined by the preferences of the nation's citizens and its political institutions, without regard for effects on other nations.

As separation fences have been lowered and technological innovations have shrunk economic distances, a multitude of formerly neglected differences among nations' domestic policies have become exposed to international scrutiny. National governments and international negotiations must thus increasingly deal with "deeper"—behind-the-border—integration. For example, if country A permits companies to emit air and water pollutants whereas country B does not, companies that use pollution-generating methods of production will find it cheaper to produce in country A. Companies in country B that compete internationally with companies in country A are likely to complain that foreign competitors enjoy unfair advantages and to press for international pollution standards.

Deeper integration requires analysis of the economic and the political aspects of virtually all nonborder policies and practices. Such issues have already figured prominently in negotiations over the evolution of the European Community, over the Uruguay Round of GATT negotiations, over the North American Free Trade Agreement (NAFTA), and over the bilateral economic relationships between Japan and the United States. Future debates about behind-the-border policies will occur with increasing frequency and prove at least as complex and contentious as the past negotiations regarding at-the-border restrictions.

Tensions about deeper integration arise from three broad sources: cross-border spillovers, diminished national autonomy, and challenges to political sovereignty.

Cross-Border Spillovers

Some activities in one nation produce consequences that spill across borders and affect other nations. Illustrations of these spillovers abound. Given the impact of modern technology of banking and securities markets in creating interconnected networks, lax rules in one nation erode the ability of all other nations to enforce banking and securities rules and to deal with fraudulent transactions. Given the rapid diffusion of knowledge, science and technology policies in one nation generate knowledge that other nations can use without full payment. Labor market policies become matters of concern to other nations because workers migrate in search of work; policies in one nation can trigger migration that floods or starves labor markets elsewhere. When one nation dumps pollutants into the air or water that other nations breathe or drink, the matter goes beyond the unitary concern of the polluting nation and becomes a matter for international negotiation. Indeed, the hydrocarbons that are emitted into the atmosphere when individual nations burn coal for generating electricity contribute to global warming and are thereby a matter of concern for the entire world.

The tensions associated with cross-border spillovers can be especially vexing when national policies generate outcomes alleged to be competitively inequitable, as in the example in which country A permits companies to emit pollutants and country B does not. Or consider a situation in which country C requires commodities, whether produced at home or abroad, to meet certain design standards, justified for safety reasons. Foreign competitors may find it too expensive to meet these standards. In that event, the standards in C act very much like tariffs or quotas, effectively narrowing or even eliminating foreign competition for domestic producers. Citing examples of this sort, producers or governments in individual nations often complain that business is not conducted on a "level playing field." Typically, the complaining nation proposes that *other* nations adjust their policies to moderate or remove the competitive inequities.

Arguments for creating a level playing field are troublesome at best. International trade occurs precisely because of differences among nations—in resource endowments, labor skills, and consumer tastes. Nations specialize in producing goods and services in which they are relatively most efficient. In a fundamental sense, cross-border trade is valuable because the playing field is *not* level.

When David Ricardo first developed the theory of comparative advantage, he focused on differences among nations owing to climate or technology. But Ricardo could as easily have ascribed the productive differences to differing "social climates" as to physical or technological climates. Taking all "climatic" differences as given, the theory of comparative advantage argues that free trade among nations will maximize global welfare.

Taken to its logical extreme, the notion of leveling the playing field implies that nations should become homogeneous in all major respects. But that recommendation is unrealistic and even pernicious. Suppose country A decides that it is too poor to afford the costs of a clean environment, and will thus permit the production of goods that pollute local air and water supplies. Or suppose it concludes that it cannot afford stringent protections for worker safety. Country A will then argue that it is inappropriate for other nations to impute to country A the value they themselves place on a clean environment and safety standards (just as it would be inappropriate to impute the A valuations to the environment of other nations). The core of the idea of political sovereignty is to permit national residents to order their lives and property in accord with their own preferences.

Which perspective about differences among nations in behind-the-border policies is more compelling? Is country A merely exercising its national preferences and appropriately exploiting its comparative advantage in goods that are dirty or dangerous to produce? Or does a legitimate international problem exist that justifies pressure from other nations urging country A to accept changes in its policies (thus curbing its national sovereignty)? When national governments negotiate resolutions to such questions—trying to agree whether individual nations are legitimately exercising sovereign choices or, alternatively, engaging in behavior that is unfair or damaging to other nations—the dialogue is invariably contentious because the resolutions depend on the typically complex circumstances of the international spillovers and on the relative weights accorded to the interests of particular individuals and particular nations.

Diminished National Autonomy

As cross-border economic integration increases, governments experience greater difficulties in trying to control events within their borders. Those difficulties, summarized by the term *diminished autonomy*, are the second set of reasons why tensions arise from the competition between political sovereignty and economic integration.

For example, nations adjust monetary and fiscal policies to influence domestic inflation and employment. In setting these policies, smaller countries have always been somewhat constrained by foreign economic events and policies. Today, however, all nations are constrained, often severely. More than in the past, therefore, nations may be better able to achieve their economic goals if they work together collaboratively in adjusting their macroeconomic policies.

Diminished autonomy and cross-border spillovers can sometimes be allowed to persist without explicit international cooperation to deal with them. States in the United States adopt their own tax systems and set policies for assistance to poor single people without any formal cooperation or limitation. Market pressures operate to force a degree of de facto cooperation. If one state taxes corporations too heavily, it knows business will move elsewhere. (Those familiar with older debates about "fiscal federalism" within the United States and other nations will recognize the similarity between those issues and the emerging international debates about deeper integration of national economies.) Analogously, differences among nations in regulations, standards, policies, institutions, and even social and cultural preferences create economic incentives for a kind of arbitrage that erodes or eliminates the differences. Such pressures involve not only the conventional arbitrage that exploits price differentials (buying at one point in geographic space or time and selling at another) but also shifts in the location of production facilities and in the residence of factors of production.

In many other cases, however, cross-border spillovers, arbitrage pressures, and diminished effectiveness of national policies can produce unwanted consequences. In cases involving what economists call externalities (external economies and diseconomies), national governments may need to cooperate to promote mutual interests. For example, population growth, continued urbanization, and the more intensive exploitation of natural resources generate external diseconomies not only within but across national boundaries. External economies generated when benefits spill across national jurisdictions probably also increase in importance (for instance, the gains from basic research and from control of communicable diseases).

None of these situations is new, but technological change and the reduction of tariffs and quotas heighten their importance. When one nation produces goods (such as scientific research) or "bads" (such as pollution) that significantly affect other nations, individual governments acting sequentially and noncooperatively cannot deal effectively with the resulting issues. In the absence of explicit cooperation and political leadership, too few collective goods and too many collective bads will be supplied.

Challenges to Political Sovereignty

The pressures from cross-border economic integration sometimes even lead individuals or governments to challenge the core assumptions of national political sovereignty. Such challenges are a third source of tensions about deeper integration.

The existing world system of nation-states assumes that a nation's residents are free to follow their own values and to select their own political arrangements without interference from others. Similarly, property rights are allocated by nation. (The so-called global commons, such as outer space and the deep seabed, are the sole exceptions.) A nation is assumed to have the sovereign right to exploit its property in accordance with its own preferences and policies. Political sovereignty is thus analogous to the concept of consumer sovereignty (the presumption that the individual consumer best knows his or her own interests and should exercise them freely).

In times of war, some nations have had sovereignty wrested from them by force. In earlier eras, a handful of individuals or groups have questioned the premises of political sovereignty. With the profound increases in economic integration in recent decades, however, a larger number of individuals and groups—and occasionally even their national governments—have identified circumstances in which, it is claimed, some universal or international set of values should take precedence over the preferences or policies of particular nations.

Some groups seize on human-rights issues, for example, or what they deem to be egregiously inappropriate political arrangements in other nations. An especially prominent case occurred when citizens in many nations labeled the former apartheid policies of South Africa an affront to universal values and emphasized

that the South African government was not legitimately representing the interests of a majority of South Africa's residents. Such views
caused many national governments to apply economic sanctions
against South Africa. Examples of value conflicts are not restricted to
human rights, however. Groups focusing on environmental issues
characterize tropical rain forests as the lungs of the world and the
genetic repository for numerous species of plants and animals that
are the heritage of all mankind. Such views lead Europeans, North
Americans, or Japanese to challenge the timber-cutting policies of
Brazilians and Indonesians. A recent controversy over tuna fishing
with long drift nets that kill porpoises is yet another example.
Environmentalists in the United States whose sensibilities were
offended by the drowning of porpoises required U.S. boats at
some additional expense to amend their fishing practices. The
U.S. fishermen, complaining about imported tuna caught with
less regard for porpoises, persuaded the U.S. government to ban
such tuna imports (both direct imports from the countries in
which the tuna is caught and indirect imports shipped via third
countries). Mexico and Venezuela were the main countries affected by this ban; a GATT dispute panel sided with Mexico
against the United States in the controversy, which further upset
the U.S. environmental community.

A common feature of all such examples is the existence, real or
alleged, of "psychological externalities" or "political failures." Those
holding such views reject untrammeled political sovereignty for nation-states in deference to universal or non-national values. They
wish to constrain the exercise of individual nations' sovereignties
through international negotiations or, if necessary, by even stronger
intervention.

The Management of International Convergence

In areas in which arbitrage pressures and cross-border spillovers
are weak and psychological or political externalities are largely
absent, national governments may encounter few problems with
deeper integration. Diversity across nations may persist quite easily. But at the other extreme, arbitrage and spillovers in some areas

may be so strong that they threaten to erode national diversity completely. Or psychological and political sensitivities may be asserted too powerfully to be ignored. Governments will then be confronted with serious tensions, and national policies and behaviors may eventually converge to common, worldwide patterns (for example, subject to internationally agreed norms or minimum standards). Eventual convergence across nations, if it occurs, could happen in a harmful way (national policies and practices being driven to a least common denominator with externalities ignored, in effect a "race to the bottom") or it could occur with mutually beneficial results ("survival of the fittest and the best").

Each study in this series addresses basic questions about the management of international convergence: if, when, and how national governments should intervene to try to influence the consequences of arbitrage pressures, cross-border spillovers, diminished autonomy, and the assertion of psychological or political externalities. A wide variety of responses is conceivable. We identify six, which should be regarded not as distinct categories but as ranges along a continuum.

National autonomy defines a situation at one end of the continuum in which national governments make decentralized decisions with little or no consultation and no explicit cooperation. This response represents political sovereignty at its strongest, undiluted by any international management of convergence.

Mutual recognition, like national autonomy, presumes decentralized decisions by national governments and relies on market competition to guide the process of international convergence. Mutual recognition, however, entails exchanges of information and consultations among governments to constrain the formation of national regulations and policies. As understood in discussions of economic integration within the European Community, moreover, mutual recognition entails an explicit acceptance by each member nation of the regulations, standards, and certification procedures of other members. For example, mutual recognition allows wine or liquor produced in any European Union country to be sold in all twelve member countries even if production standards in member countries differ. Doctors licensed in France are permitted to practice in

Germany, and vice versa, even if licensing procedures in the two countries differ.

Governments may agree on rules that restrict their freedom to set policy or that promote gradual convergence in the structure of policy. As international consultations and monitoring of compliance with such rules become more important, this situation can be described as *monitored decentralization.* The Group of Seven finance ministers meetings, supplemented by the IMF's surveillance over exchange rate and macroeconomic policies, illustrate this approach to management.

Coordination goes further than mutual recognition and monitored decentralization in acknowledging convergence pressures. It is also more ambitious in promoting intergovernmental cooperation to deal with them. Coordination involves jointly designed mutual adjustments of national policies. In clear-cut cases of coordination, bargaining occurs and governments agree to behave differently from the ways they would have behaved without the agreement. Examples include the World Health Organization's procedures for controlling communicable diseases and the 1987 Montreal Protocol (to a 1985 framework convention) for the protection of stratospheric ozone by reducing emissions of chlorofluorocarbons.

Explicit harmonization, which requires still higher levels of intergovernmental cooperation, may require agreement on regional standards or world standards. Explicit harmonization typically entails still greater departures from decentralization in decisionmaking and still further strengthening of international institutions. The 1988 agreement among major central banks to set minimum standards for the required capital positions of commercial banks (reached through the Committee on Banking Regulations and Supervisory Practices at the Bank for International Settlements) is an example of partially harmonized regulations.

At the opposite end of the spectrum from national autonomy lies *federalist mutual governance,* which implies continuous bargaining and joint, centralized decisionmaking. To make federalist mutual governance work would require greatly strengthened supranational institutions. This end of the management spectrum,

now relevant only as an analytical benchmark, is a possible outcome that can be imagined for the middle or late decades of the
twenty-first century, possibly even sooner for regional groupings
like the European Union.

Overview of the Brookings Project

Despite their growing importance, the issues of deeper economic
integration and its competition with national political sovereignty
were largely neglected in the 1980s. In 1992 the Brookings Institution initiated its project on Integrating National Economies to direct
attention to these important questions.

In studying this topic, Brookings sought and received the
cooperation of some of the world's leading economists, political
scientists, foreign-policy specialists, and government officials,
representing all regions of the world. Although some functional
areas require a special focus on European, Japanese, and North
American perspectives, at all junctures the goal was to include,
in addition, the perspectives of developing nations and the formerly centrally planned economies.

The first phase of the project commissioned the twenty-one
scholarly studies listed at the beginning of the book. One or two
lead discussants, typically residents of parts of the world other
than the area where the author resides, were asked to comment
on each study.

Authors enjoyed substantial freedom to design their individual
studies, taking due account of the overall themes and goals of the
project. The guidelines for the studies requested that at least some
of the analysis be carried out with a non-normative perspective. In
effect, authors were asked to develop a "baseline" of what might
happen in the absence of changed policies or further international
cooperation. For their normative analyses, authors were asked to
start with an agnostic posture that did not prejudge the net benefits or costs resulting from integration. The project organizers
themselves had no presumption about whether national diversity is
better or worse than international convergence or about what the
individual studies should conclude regarding the desirability of

increased integration. On the contrary, each author was asked to address the trade-offs in his or her issue area between diversity and convergence and to locate the area, currently and prospectively, on the spectrum of international management possibilities running between national autonomy through mutual recognition to coordination and explicit harmonization.

HENRY J. AARON   SUSAN M. COLLINS
RALPH C. BRYANT   ROBERT Z. LAWRENCE

Chapter 1

Introduction

THE GOVERNANCE structures of limited liability companies encompass the relationships among management, stockholders, creditors, employees, suppliers, and customers. These structures differ from country to country, even though the countries, such as the members of the Organization for Economic Cooperation and Development, may generally be characterized as having market economies. In recent years, increased international integration of economic activities has heightened awareness of these cross-country differences in corporate governance structure and in the structure of financial markets.

In the late 1980s a wave of direct investment from Japan to the United States, particularly acquisitions of U.S. companies by Japanese firms, pointed up the relative lack of foreign acquisitions of Japanese companies. Meanwhile, tighter economic integration in the European Community was affecting the core characteristics of economic institutions in member countries, including the way companies are governed. Increasing integration of financial markets in Europe is forcing EC (now European Union) member governments to further harmonize rules for financial markets. Intensifying international competition among multinational corporations has also drawn attention to differences among countries in the cost of capital. Finally, the increasing cross-border investments have provided first-hand experience for both investors and issuers of equity on the variations in relations among shareholders, creditors, and the management of companies in different countries.

1

The international diversification of portfolios has been driven by both supply and demand. Issuers of equity have encouraged internationalization of their investor base as a means of improving liquidity and lowering the costs of capital. Investors have sought more stable returns through portfolio diversification. More and more investors have thus become aware of variations from country to country in the rules of investment, including disclosure requirements, the voting power of shareholders, restraints on insider trading, laws regulating acquisitions, and bankruptcy codes.

Meanwhile, the increasing output of Japanese automakers in the United States and the United Kingdom has drawn attention to a manufacturing system that can achieve higher productivity and better quality than many of its competitors. Although first characterized as an efficient inventory management system—just-in-time delivery—or a flexible labor management system, Japanese production was gradually recognized as a new and efficient way of manufacturing. Now known as a lean production system as opposed to the traditional mass production system, this mode of manufacturing involves more skilled assembly workers with more training, closer manufacturer cooperation with a smaller number of large suppliers, less vertical integration of production, drastically smaller inventories, a greater variety of products made on one assembly line, and continuous improvements in productivity and quality through active participation of assembly workers. One indispensable requirement of the lean production system has been a large number of employees covered by implicit long-term contracts who are deeply committed to the well-being of their company.

The relationship of companies supplying a major assembler such as Toyota, Nissan, or Honda is usually called a *production keiretsu* (a Japanese word for a series of things organized to perform a function). Transactions among companies in a keiretsu are most often based on long-term implicit contracts instead of being ordinary arm's-length transactions.[1] Japanese automakers in the United States and the United Kingdom have wanted to establish

---

1. The negotiations between Japan and the United States under the Structural Impediments Initiative (SII), begun in 1989 and completed in 1990, included an item related to this keiretsu relationship.

similar relationships with local suppliers, which would require a very high level of cooperation from them to improve quality and productivity. The relationships have been criticized by some U.S. observers as anticompetitive and have incited complaints from perplexed suppliers who faced such exacting demands for the first time. Long-term implicit contracts also require credible long-term commitments by the management of companies, commitments that are often difficult for American and British companies to make. But the merit of the Japanese contractual system has gradually been recognized.[2] And as understanding of the Japanese economy has deepened, Japanese corporate governance structure has attracted attention.

As Japanese manufacturers began to show their strength in international markets, potential problems in the governance of U.S. corporations were brought to light. When President Bush visited Japan in 1992 with executives of American auto companies, the high compensation of U.S. top executives attracted strong attention; top executives of Japanese auto companies are rewarded far less lavishly than their American counterparts in spite of the superior performance of Japanese companies. In addition, the short time horizons of U.S. managers, the possible deleterious effects of mergers and acquisitions on the long-term viability of U.S. companies, and the massive layoffs of white-collar workers in the recession of 1991–92 all drew public attention to problems in U.S. corporate governance.[3]

Meanwhile, Japan has become increasingly aware of the weaknesses in its own system of corporate governance. It is, for example, very difficult for a new company to break into a market and grow rapidly in the network of long-term relationships that binds established companies together. This difficulty in penetrating Japanese markets has been heavily criticized as a trade barrier by foreign countries. And in the labor market, traditional corporate governance demands long working hours from employees and

2. See Womack, Jones, and Roos (1990); and Dertouzos and others (1989).

3. The collapse of communist economies, especially the spectacular failure of state enterprises, also illuminated the importance of adequate corporate governance in modern economies.

routinely requires that they move to distant assignments with little notice, often having to leave their families behind. Although these demands are recognized as a cost of job security, many people are beginning to question the trade-off between family life and loyalty to their companies. Finally, a rigid accounting system inhibits transactions that are off the balance sheet and distorts reported profits. Many companies, including Japanese banks, are setting up foreign subsidiaries to circumvent these problems.

All these developments have not only increased awareness of the importance of corporate governance but have generated pressures to alter the institutional framework in which companies operate. Furthermore, large companies that have traditionally limited share-holding to domestic investors are now courting foreign investors to lower their cost of equity. This internationalization of the investor base has put pressure on companies to disclose their accounts on an internationally comparable basis.

International Differences in Corporate Governance

This study compares the institutional differences in the gover-nance of large corporations in five major industrial countries: the United States, Japan, Germany, France, and the United Kingdom. Superficially, the structures of limited liability companies are sim-ilar: the shareholders elect the directors by a simple majority (except in Germany, where the shareholders choose half the mem-bers of the powerful supervisory board and employees choose the other half). However, institutional details are often very important in determining the companies' behavior. In Japan, Germany, and France shareholders may get involved in the management of com-panies rather easily if they choose to do so. They have stronger voting rights and face fewer restrictions in communicating among themselves and with management than shareholders do in the United States and the United Kingdom. In the United States and the United Kingdom, shareholders cannot become involved so easily in management without taking over a company. Sharehold-ers of U.S. companies, for example, cannot nominate directors to boards through a regular proxy process, and they cannot make a binding decision on executive compensation. Under the very strict U.S. insider trading rules, shareholders cannot communicate with the management informally about investment projects and other important issues.

The strong voting power of shareholders in Japanese and German companies and the better communication between them and management seem to have forged more stable ownership. Cross-shareholding among companies with business relationships is important in Japan. Many German companies have concentrated and stable owners. And Japanese and German banks are often large shareholders of companies in their countries. The ownership of U.S. and U.K. companies is less concentrated and stable than it is in Japan and Germany, and financial institutions interested only in investment are among the largest shareholders. As a result, the stock markets in the United States and the United Kingdom play the role of the market for corporate control, but management in Japanese and German companies is more stable and can offer more credible commitment than can management in American and British companies.

The role of capital also varies from country to country. The restrictions on cash payments to shareholders so as to maintain the net assets of a company corresponding to its paid-in capital are much stricter in Japan, Germany, and France than in the United States. The rules in the United Kingdom used to be similar to those in the United States, but are more in line with those in Japan, Germany, and France since Britain joined the European Community. Accounting systems, partly based on the historical cost of capturing assets, in Germany, Japan, and France have generally measured earnings and assets more conservatively in the long run than have accounting systems in the United States and the United Kingdom. As a result, in Japan, Germany, and France the paid-in capital is traditionally regarded as security for creditors and other stakeholders of the company rather than as the property of shareholders.

These differences in corporate structure have many implications for the performance of companies. The cost of capital and the effective use of employees are affected by the structure. The strength of the rights of shareholders is likely to affect the cost of equity. A stock that carries a strong voting power commands a higher price than one with weak voting power because strong voting power enables stockholders to influence the management more readily. Strong restrictions on cash distributions to shareholders lower the cost of debt and allow companies to maintain greater leverage because creditors are not so likely to face sudden reductions in company equity. But the same restrictions may also raise the cost of equity because shareholders have less control on cash held by the company. As for employee relations, it is easier for the management of Japanese and German companies than it is for the management of U.S. and U.K. companies to maintain long-term implicit contracts with employees But although this stability may allow Japanese and German companies to invest more in firm-specific job training, it also makes redeployment of people from declining sectors to growing ones more difficult.

The Future of Corporate Governance Structures

Financial structures, as well as corporate governance structures have been pushed toward greater uniformity. Financial authorities have been pressured to adopt stricter rules to protect small shareholders and to avoid manipulations of the market by corporate insiders. Shareholders have wanted to have rules to treat all shareholders equally, and national authorities have competed to have efficient and trusted national financial markets so as to promote securities trading. These pressures have achieved some convergence in regulations on insider trading and acquisitions.

At present, considerable differences among countries remain in disclosure and accounting rules. However, more frequent cross-border transactions involving securities have created market pressures for more uniform rules. Companies that have an increasingly multinational investor base face pressures from their creditors and shareholders to disclose their performance on a more internationally comparable basis. And firms that want to reduce their cost of funds by attracting more investors find that it is to their advantage to have internationally comparable disclosure statements. As a result, more comparable disclosure rules are evolving, which is desirable for the more efficient allocation of capital. Policymakers can assist and accelerate this convergence.

Bankruptcy procedures also differ across countries. Because bankruptcy rules sometimes override private contracts for orderly rehabilitation or liquidation of failing companies, they affect the rights of creditors and shareholders. As international financial transactions expand, it would be desirable to harmonize bankruptcy procedures in various countries to reduce the legal risks involved in these transactions. Market pressure alone is not sufficient to achieve this convergence, however, given the slow progress to date. The Organization for Economic Cooperation and Development and other international organizations could become catalysts for convergence by presenting a model bankruptcy law.

Regarding the more fundamental aspects of corporate governance, such as the voting rights of shareholders and the role of paid-in capital, piecemeal harmonization of individual components of the various structures is not desirable because they generally form consistent systems. For example, it would be very difficult to have an open market for corporate control of established large companies in Japan or in Germany. Given the implicit long-term contracts in these companies, a sudden change of management would likely result in a breach of contracts by the new management. One possible remedy is to convert implicit long-term contracts to more explicit and transparent contracts to allow a more contestable market of corporate control. However, in practice, this conversion would be almost impossible to achieve.

Given the different advantages of various corporate governance systems and their deep-rooted institutional backgrounds, it is neither desirable nor feasible to adopt a single model of governance as the world standard. Market pressures for convergence may even produce perverse results. Because the current national regulatory structure allows regulatory arbitrage among jurisdictions by the management of companies, the competition among national authorities to attract companies may result in distorted corporate governance that is biased toward entrenched management. The state control of corporate law in the United States allows such arbitrages: the directors can effectively change a company's corporate charter without shareholders' approval by lobbying for a change in the state corporate law. The European Union may face similar problems. These problems may become more serious as equity portfolios diversify across national borders.

Rather, each country should allow various forms of corporate governance for companies established in its territory. In each form there should be a good balance of power among shareholders, boards of directors, and other stakeholders. A country could, for instance, have several models of corporate governance in its corporate law: the U.S. model, the Japanese model, and the German model. (In fact, French law allows two types of corporate structures: the traditional single-tier board structure and the German two-tier structure.) At the time of incorporation a company could choose the one that best suits its purpose, and it would have to disclose its structure to its stakeholders. A venture company might want to choose the U.S. model, which allows very flexible restructuring in its paid-in capital. A manufacturing company might adopt the Japanese or German model, both of which are more conducive to stable management.

The law that provides this menu approach might allow a company to change its organizational model. As the company grows, its activities could change and it might want to adopt a different structure. But any such reorganization should not unduly disrupt the contractual relationships among its stakeholders. A change of corporate model should require the approval of its shareholders with a majority at least equal to that required for any other change in the articles of incorporation. If a change would weaken restrictions on payouts to shareholders, the company should obtain the approval of creditors as well.

There is no single ideal system of corporate governance, and the search for a better system will continue. But although a country has to choose one system for national governance, it does not have to do so for corporate governance. A menu of structures would create competition among companies that should result in more efficient corporate structures for various kinds of business activities.

Chapter 2

Limited Liability Companies in Modern Economies

*E*ARLY limited liability companies were established by special authorization of the government. During the nineteenth century, entrepreneurs in the United Kingdom, France, Germany, and many other countries were allowed without special permission to establish companies with transferable shares and limited liability. In the United States limited liability was recognized state by state. New Hampshire first allowed it in manufacturing in 1816; California allowed it only in 1931.[1] Japan, which imported German corporate law, adopted its first commercial code allowing free establishment of limited liability companies in 1899.[2]

The organizational principle of a limited liability company has been the driving force of economic development in the industrialized countries. These corporations invest in physical and human capital by raising funds, issuing shares and debts, and employing workers. In recent years the importance of the corporate contribution has been dramatically demonstrated by the collapse of the centrally planned economies of eastern Europe and the Soviet Union.

Advantages and Disadvantages of Limited Liability

In modern economies, production processes and distribution systems are often too large and expensive for an individual or a

1. Namiki (1989, pp. 4–12).
2. Kishida (1991, pp. 46–49).

9

small group of investors to own. Laws for limited liability companies provide a convenient legal framework for organizing large business operations because they allow partial ownership of the business by a number of investors.

The ingenuity of the limited liability system is that it allows investors to sell or buy shares without paying much attention to the identities or wealth of other shareholders. In partnerships, each partner is liable for the debts of the partnership. When all partners are rich, there is less likelihood that any one partner will incur a large amount of debt. Thus the potential liability of a partner depends crucially on the personal wealth of the other partners. The transfer of a partner's equity always requires the consent of all the partners. But the responsibility of the shareholders of a limited liability company is already discharged when a fully paid share is issued. As a result, the potential loss from investment is limited. These characteristics greatly facilitate the transfer of ownership, and the shares of most large companies are freely transferable. Thus a limited liability company will reduce the cost of capital by making the share more liquid and by allowing diversification of risk for investors. The shares of large companies are often traded in organized stock exchanges in which investors can buy and sell shares freely.[3]

The shareholders of a company usually elect the directors, who are in charge of managing the business. This mechanism allows infinite life for firms by separating ownership from management. Most persons who are capable of managing a company do not have the money to own it entirely. The legal framework of limited liability companies allows the shareholders of a company to choose its managers irrespective of the managers' wealth.

But limited liability companies also have some disadvantages. Because of the limited risk, shareholders have an incentive to take excessive business risks and to pass the risks to creditors if the company incurs debts (the so-called moral hazard). By undertaking a risky but potentially highly profitable investment, share-

---

3. See chapter 2 of Easterbrook and Fischel (1991) for a detailed discussion on the merits of limited liability of shareholders.

holders can obtain all the gains with limited stakes, but the creditors only get predetermined interest with the possibility of losing the principal. Although some creditors such as banks and bondholders can protect their interest by loan agreements or bond covenants, these mechanisms are often too cumbersome for employees, and suppliers, and other small creditors.

Again, given the limited liability of shareholders, the only security for employees, suppliers, and other creditors is the assets of the company corresponding to the legal (stated) capital. In most countries a company can pay dividends to its shareholders only when its net assets exceed the amount of its legal capital. Therefore, the accounting rules on the evaluation of net assets have to strike a balance between the shareholders and a company's other stakeholders. The accounting system and disclosure system of the accounts of a company have been developed to take care of this problem, but the evaluation of assets is often very difficult and cannot eliminate some arbitrary elements.

Large companies without large shareholders may also have problems monitoring and disciplining the management. The managers of a company possess inside information about it and may try to use the information to advance their own interests at the cost of other stakeholders, especially shareholders. These activities include trading securities on the basis of inside information, excessive undisclosed compensation for executives, lucrative transactions between management and company, and so forth. Monitoring management can be serious for large companies with dispersed ownership of shares, because small shareholders are generally not interested in the operation of the company.[4] When the equity of a company is held widely, no single shareholder thinks that he is important enough to affect the management. Even if a shareholder tries to monitor and improve the management of the company, any gain from his activities is shared by all shareholders. So there is a strong incentive for each shareholder to be a free rider and leave monitoring to somebody else.

---

4. This incentive problem related to the separation of ownership and management of a company is usually called the problem of agency cost. See Stiglitz (1985) and Rubin (1990, pp. 73–93), for example.

International Differences in Corporate Governance Structures

To maximize the advantages provided by limited liability companies while controlling the potential problems, each country has developed its own governance structure for them. In some ways, the designs of governance for limited liability companies are similar to those of democratic governments. For each company, the national company law (state company law in the United States) and its articles of incorporation are like the constitution of a national state. Shareholders can usually vote to appoint and dismiss directors and can be asked by the board of directors to approve important business decisions, including changes in the articles of incorporation. Broadly within this framework, decision-making power can be allocated between shareholders and the board of directors. But as in democracies, the precise forms the allocations take vary significantly.

This chapter discusses important differences in corporate governance in the United States, Japan, Germany, France, and the United Kingdom. Although I cover many of the important aspects of corporate governance structure, this discussion is by no means comprehensive. I do not, for example, discuss the application of antitrust policy, labor relations laws, and government ownership of the corporate sector. The appendix provides comparative descriptions of the important institutional differences in corporate governance.

Board of Directors: One-Tier Structure

The directors of limited liability companies in the United States, Japan, France, and the United Kingdom are elected by a simple majority of the shareholders. In large German companies, shareholders choose half the members of the powerful supervisory board and employees choose the other half. However, in practice, there are a number of variations stemming from the details of the institutional arrangements.

In the United States, Japan, France, and the United Kingdom the shareholders directly elect the members of the board of directors, who are responsible for managing the company—a single-tier board.[5] In the United States, Japan, and the United Kingdom the members of the board of directors are elected for relatively short periods (usually one to three years in the United States, two years in Japan, and three years in the United Kingdom). In France directors' terms are set by a company's articles of incorporation and can be as long as six years. In most U.S. companies the shareholders can remove a director (with or without cause, depending on the articles of incorporation) by a simple majority vote. In Japan a two-thirds majority of shareholders can dismiss a director with or without cause (in the latter case, with compensation). In France, a director can be dismissed by a simple majority vote of the shareholders. In the United Kingdom, members of the board can be removed by the shareholders with a simple majority vote, possibly after payment of compensation.

Board of Directors: Two-Tier Structure

Although company laws allow the directors to manage the company themselves in these four countries, many directors are not involved in full-time management. In large U.S. companies, often the chairman of the board and a few other directors, along with officers chosen by the board, manage the firm. This is also the case with large French companies: the chairman of the board and the executive officers (who need not necessarily be directors) are appointed by the board and are responsible for the general management. In these countries the role of the board of directors is usually limited to one of control; most members attend the board meetings only to monitor the management. These members are called outside directors because they are not full-time managers of the firm and are hired from outside the company. Most members of the boards of Japanese companies, however, are executive directors who manage their firms full time and are usually promoted

---

5. French companies can choose a German-style two-tier board structure, but most are organized as traditional single-tier companies.

Table 2-1. *Directors Promoted from among Employees, Japan and United States, 1986*

Percent of directors promoted from among employees	Percent of companies surveyed	
	Japanese companies	*U.S. companies*
100	19.9	5.2
80–100	39.2	6.2
60–80	22.2	8.3
40–60	11.7	15.4
0–40	7.0	64.9

Source: Kishida (1994, p. 179).

from middle management (table 2-1). An average of 77.8 percent of Japanese directors are promoted from among employees; in the United States 35.1 percent are from among employees. The structure of the boards of British companies is diverse; although most have some outside directors on the board, the number differs considerably across companies.[6] Among these four countries only in France does company law require that employee representatives attend all meetings of the board of directors in an advisory capacity.

In these four countries the legal arrangements in principle allow shareholders to replace a member of the board of directors at short notice. However, the relative power of shareholders to influence the management differs a great deal depending on the details of the institutional arrangements.

German corporations have a two-tier structure of management. In companies with more than 2,000 employees, shareholders elect half the supervisory board and employees elect the other half. Because the shareholders choose the chairman, who can cast a tiebreaking vote, they usually have the greater influence on the board. However, formal labor representation in management is by far the strongest among the five countries. Employees may remove their representatives with a three-quarters majority vote, and shareholders may also remove theirs with a three-quarters majority.

6. See Sheridan and Kendall (1992, pp. 29–51).

The supervisory board appoints the board of managing directors for a maximum term of five years (renewable). The board of managing directors manages the company on its own responsibility and represents it externally. A member of the board of managing directors may be dismissed only by the supervisory board and only for a serious reason, such as gross neglect of duty. No one can be a member of both the board of managing directors and the supervisory board of the same company. The supervisory board meets two to four times a year and usually depends on information from the managing board to monitor the activities of the company.

French corporate law introduced the German-style two-tier structure in 1966, but most companies in France remain managed by a single board of directors.[7] In French companies with the two-tier structure, the members of the supervisory board are appointed by the shareholders' meeting; employees cannot elect members. Representatives of the workers' committee are, however, entitled to attend all meetings of the supervisory board in an advisory capacity. The supervisory board appoints the members of the executive board, which manages the corporation, and monitors the action of the executive board without taking part in the conduct of the corporation's affairs. The shareholders' meeting can remove a member of the supervisory board by a simple majority vote. But a member of the executive board may be removed only by a resolution of a shareholders' meeting on the proposal of the supervisory board. In both German and French two-tier systems, the board of managing directors is more insulated from the direct pressures of shareholders than it is in the one-tier structure.

Shareholders' Voting Power and Management Influence

There are a number of important differences among countries in the power shareholders are given in the voting process by

---

7. The aborted Renault-Volvo Automotive planned to adopt a French company with a two-tier board structure (John Ridding, "The Renault-Volvo Merger: A Marriage to Respect Sensitivities," *Financial Times*, September 7, 1993, p. 28). This structure was chosen to balance the interests of Renault and Volvo. As of January 1, 1989, 137,286 French companies had adopted the single-tier structure and 1,310 the two-tier structure. See Ripert and Roblot (1991).

corporate law and other regulations (see the appendix). In Japan a relatively small shareholder can nominate candidates for the board of directors, and in Germany a shareholder can nominate candidates for the supervisory board and can publicize the nominations in the proxy form distributed by the company.[8] U.S. shareholders cannot offer their own candidates for directors' seats through the regular shareholder proposal process, and they have to finance their own proxy campaign, which can be very expensive. In the United Kingdom a shareholder has to have at least 5 percent of a company's stock to propose a candidate. In France shareholders are free to dismiss any director of the board (in the case of one-tier structures) or any member of the supervisory board (in the case of German-style, two-tier boards) by a resolution with a simple majority and can appoint a new director even if this matter is not on the agenda of the meeting.

Nominating candidates for the board of directors in Japan or the supervisory board in Germany is relatively easy, but it is difficult in the United States and the United Kingdom. As a result, in Japan and Germany large shareholders can change the makeup of the board directly when it is deemed necessary, whereas in the United States and the United Kingdom, it is often necessary to take over the company to rectify bad management.

Shareholders must approve the level of compensation for the members of the board of directors (or the supervisory board) in Japan, Germany, and France. In Japan the directors, who are also the employees of the company, are remunerated both as employees and as directors. The compensation as employees can be determined by the board of directors and can be used to circumvent control by the shareholders. In Germany, compensation of the members of the supervisory board is determined by the shareholders and compensation of the managing board by the supervisory board. German corporate law also stipulates that the compensation of the members of the supervisory and the managing boards must be reasonable and in line with the financial situation of the

---

8. This nomination power has been used infrequently in Japan. However, before the annual shareholders' meeting, management usually consults with large shareholders on new candidates for the board.

company. In France the total compensation for directors (traditional board) or members of the supervisory board (two-tier board) is decided by the annual shareholders' meeting. In two-tier boards the compensation of the executive board members is decided by the supervisory board.

In the United States a board of directors usually decides its own compensation without shareholders' approval. In many large public companies the compensation is determined by a compensation committee, which is composed entirely of outside directors. However, because two-thirds of outside directors in the United States are themselves chief executives of other companies, they have little incentive to control the compensation of the top executives of the boards for which they serve as outside directors.[9] Until 1992, U.S. companies did not have to fully disclose executive compensation. But after a change in Securities and Exchange Commission rules, the shareholders of U.S. companies can now propose a nonbinding vote on executive compensation, and the companies have to disclose their executive compensation more fully.

In the United Kingdom a company's articles of association usually stipulate that the remuneration of the directors shall be determined by a shareholders' meeting. A director may, however, also hold a salaried position in the company under an employment contract. In this case the salary under the contract is decided by the board of directors.

Compensation of top executives is important in light of its absolute level and its relationship to the performance of the company. Available evidence indicates that U.S. top executives earn much more than their Japanese counterparts. The compensation of British executives is between these two and somewhat closer to the Japanese level. The total compensation (including tax and bonuses) of the top executive of a Japanese company is six to eight times that of the most highly paid blue-collar worker. In U.S. companies the compensation of the top executive is twelve to eighteen times that of the most highly paid blue-collar worker,

9. "Bosses' Pay: Worthy of His Hire? "*Economist,* February 1, 1992, p. 19.

excluding bonuses and stock options.[10] A study by Graef Crystal found that "chief executives at top American companies earned 109 times the pay of the average American workers in the late 1980s. This compares with just 17 times in Japan and about 35 times in the U.K."[11] Other recent studies indicate that U.S. CEOs receive about twice to three and one-half times as much money as Japanese managers.[12] Although it is difficult to evaluate the compensation of top executives against their contribution to the earnings of the company, controls on executive compensation are apparently looser in U.S. companies. Using data from the 1980s, Steven Kaplan has found that compensation of top management of the largest Japanese and U.S. companies reflects such yardsticks as stock performance, sales growth, and changes in pretax corporate income in similar ways. The compensation in Japan is, however, more sensitive to falling earnings than it is in the United States.[13] Kaplan did not include long-term incentive packages such as stock options in his examination of compensation of U.S. executives, but in a study of the compensation of 955 U.S. chief executives Graef Crystal found that the correlation between the value of long-term incentive schemes and the company's performance was negative.[14] In comparing the sensitivity of executive compensation to corporate performance, one also needs to take account of the income fluctuations for other labor groups. Although the standard deviation of compensation changes of U.S. executives is comparable to that of randomly selected workers, the executives are less likely than workers to receive pay cuts and more likely to obtain raises.[15]

A recent study of the salaries plus bonuses of the highest paid directors in the largest U.K. companies showed a weak relationship

---

10. Aoki (1992). In Japanese companies, stock options are rarely included in the compensation for top management, partly because the companies are forbidden to hold their own shares except in very exceptional circumstances.

11. Quoted in Martin Dickson, "A Check on the Boss's Cheque," *Financial Times*, March 31, 1992, p. 20.

12. Kaplan (1993a, p. 17).

13. Kaplan (1993a, 1993b).

14. "Bosses' Pay," *Economist*, February 1, 1992, p. 19.

15. Jensen and Murphy (1990).

between executive compensation and corporate performance.[16] Directors' remuneration grew about 20 percent a year between 1983 and 1991 and was very weakly linked to performance. Even this relationship broke down after 1988; top directors received very high pay in the recessionary period up to 1991.

Steven Kaplan has analyzed the relationship between the turnover of top executives of largest companies in the United States, Japan, and Germany in relation to their companies' stock performance, sales growth, net income, and changes in pretax income in the 1980s.[17] Poor stock returns and income losses increased the likelihood of top management turnover to roughly the same extent and magnitude in all three countries. The turnover of Japanese top executives was more sensitive to earnings than was the turnover of U.S. top executives. But turnover in the United States was more sensitive to poor stock performance. Poor stock returns were also associated with appointments of outside directors (generally unrelated to banks or large shareholders) in the United States, appointments of directors affiliated with banks and corporate shareholders in Japan, and appointments of new supervisory board members in Germany.

Just as they have little say on levels of executive compensation, in the United States the shareholders of a publicly traded company cannot dictate to its management on issues related to business judgment. Although this is also usually the case for Japanese companies, shareholders can amend the articles of incorporation by a two-thirds majority to allow them to have binding votes on issues related to business judgment. German corporate law stipulates that the executive board alone is responsible for managing the firm and is subject to no instructions; the shareholders are, in principle, excluded from the management of the company.

16. David Goodhart, "Pay and Performance Unrelated," *Financial Times,* November 28–29, 1992, p. 5.

17. Kaplan (1993a, 1993b) compared the turnover of U.S. executive directors, Japanese representative directors, German managing directors, and German members of supervisory boards. He also compared the turnover of U.S. chief executive officers, Japanese presidents, German chairmen of boards of managing directors, and German chairmen of supervisory boards.

Shareholders' power may sometimes be limited by restrictions on the transferability of publicly traded shares or on voting power. Restrictions on transferability are generally weak in the five countries. However, boards of directors of U.S. companies sometimes restrict the transfer of shares in the event of a possible takeover by invoking the so-called poison pill defense. The defense usually involves issuing options or other securities to shareholders who can exercise them only after a triggering event such as a tender offer. The securities are designed to make acquiring a target company very expensive unless its board of directors consents. In Germany and France, companies listed on the stock exchanges cannot restrict the transferability of bearer shares, and most shares of listed companies are bearer shares. Listed companies may, however, limit transferability of registered shares through provisions in their articles of incorporation.

Shares without voting rights or with restricted voting rights are rare, or not permitted, for publicly traded shares in the United States, Japan, and the United Kingdom, except for preferred shares. In Germany and France, companies may, through their articles of incorporation, limit the voting power of an individual shareholder (to a certain percentage of a company's shares) irrespective of the number of shares held. A number of large German companies, including Mannesmann (5 percent), Deutsche Bank (5 percent), BASF and Bayer (5 percent), have this limit on voting rights.[18] In France, shareholders who have held shares for a specified period (two years, for instance) may be entitled to double votes by a company's articles of incorporation.

Ownership and the Role of Large Shareholders

Statistics on the distribution of share ownership and other evidence indicate that companies in the United States and the United Kingdom have more fragmented and less stable ownership structures than those of Japan, Germany, and France. First, the number of listed companies and the size of their capitalization relative to the size of the economy are much greater in the United States and

---

18. Schmalenbach (1990).

Table 2-2. *Number of Listed Companies and Market Capitalization of Domestic Equity as Percent of GDP, Five Countries, 1990*

Country	Listed domestic companies	Market capitalization of quoted equity (percent of GDP)
United States[a]	6,342	56.5
Japan[b]	1,627	88.5
Germany	649	23.3
France[c]	443	25.8
United Kingdom	2,006	80.8

Source: Mayer (1993, graphs 1 and 2).
a. Total companies on New York Stock Exchange, NASDAQ, and American Exchange.
b. Total companies on Tokyo Stock Exchange.
c. Total companies on Paris Stock Exchange.

the United Kingdom than they are in France and Germany (table 2-2). The ownership base of privately held companies is, by definition, much narrower and more stable than is that of publicly traded companies. Japan has a large number of listed companies and large capitalization, but most Japanese listed companies have a very stable ownership structure.

Tables 2-3 and 2-4 show the distribution of share ownership in the five countries. Data for the United States in table 2-3 are adjusted by removing the estimated holdings of corporations and individuals who base their trades on broker recommendations. The figures thus separate shareholders who are managing their portfolios as agents for others from owners who are managing their own money. In table 2-4 the usual institutional classification of ownership is used to show the distribution of shareholders. These tables also show that the percentage of shares owned by pension funds, mutual funds, and other institutional investors is very large in the United States (55 to 60 percent) and the United Kingdom (about 60 percent). One of the reasons for this dominance is the large size of private pension funds. In Japan, Germany, and France the state pension contributions are relatively high and private pension funds are consequently much less important.[19]

---

19. According to Davis (1992, tables 1 and 2), the assets of pension funds relative to GDP in 1990 are as follows: United States, 35 percent; Japan, 5 percent; Germany, 3 percent; France, 3 percent (in 1988); United Kingdom, 55 percent.

Table 2-3. *Stock Ownership in U.S., Japanese, and German Industry, by Type of Owner, 1991–92*

Percent

Owner	United States[a]	Japan[b]	Germany[c]
Domestic individuals	30–35	20	4
Institutional owners	2	40	27
Institutional agents	55–60	6	3
Corporations	2–7	30	41
Government	Negligible	Negligible	6
Foreign investors	6	4	19

Source: Porter (1992).

a. Official ownership data have been adjusted by removing estimated holdings of corporations and individuals who fully base their trades on broker recommendations. Data for institutional owners include estimated holdings of insurance companies for their own accounts.

b. Some of the shares held by Japanese financial institutions are traded rapidly.

c. Total for institutional owners includes stock owned by individuals but held and voted by German banks (14 percent of total).

Table 2-4. *Ownership of Publicly Listed Corporations in Four Countries, by Sector, 1990–91*

Percent

Owner	United States	Japan	Germany	United Kingdom
Financial sector				
Banks[a]	0.3	25.2	8.9	0.9
Insurance companies	5.2	17.3	10.6	18.4
Pension funds[b]	24.8	0.9	. . .	30.4
Investment companies and other	9.5	3.6	. . .	11.1
Total	39.8	47.0	19.5	60.8
Nonfinancial sector				
Nonfinancial businesses	. . .	25.1	39.2	3.6
Households	53.5	23.1	16.8	21.3
Government	. . .	0.6	6.8	2.0
Foreign	6.7	4.2	17.7	12.3

Source: Kester (1992, table 4).

a. All types, including bank holding companies.

b. Public and private.

Finally, pension funds in the United States and the United Kingdom behave as fund managers of the beneficiary that have a narrow focus on maximizing the short-term return of their portfolios. As a result they are often blamed for their very short-term trading of shares.[20] This is partly because, in the United States, antitrust regulations, tax codes, rules on the proxy process, rules preventing insider trading, takeover defense measures taken by the management, and other factors strongly discourage institutional investors from behaving as active owners of companies and interacting with management (box 2-1).[21] With all these obstacles, it is no wonder that institutional investors prefer to sell their shares of weaker performers than to try to be actively involved in corporate governance.

U.S. rules on insider trading require special discussion. Because stock markets developed early in the industrialization of the United States and played an important part in financing emerging firms, the protection of small investors became a significant administrative concern. To avoid giving unfair advantages to large shareholders, tight restrictions on insider trading were introduced at an early stage. However, these restrictions made it difficult for management to transmit sensitive information on a firm to large shareholders informally (the appendix describes the current regulations on insider trading). Compared with rules in the other four countries, U.S. rules apply more severe penalties to violators. Moreover, their wording is ambiguous, and court interpretations of their application have differed. As a result, there is a great deal of uncertainty about the extent to which investors can communicate with the management without violating the rule.

Shareholding in a given company by other companies that have long-term relationships with it is much more common in Japan and Germany than in the United States and the United Kingdom. In Japan cross-shareholdings among companies that share main

---

20. According to Froot, Perold, and Stein (1991, table 1), U.S. pension funds and mutual funds had a time horizon (reciprocal of percent turnover) of about two years.

21. The California Public Employees Retirement System (CalPERS) is actively monitoring the performance of some companies in its portfolio. However, this is the exception rather than the norm. See Jacobs (1991, pp. 55–56).

Box 2-1. *Factors Discouraging U.S. Institutional Shareholders from Behaving as Active Investors*

Hart-Scott-Rodino Act of 1976. In this major antitrust law, the Federal Trade Commission stipulates that the following activities could be viewed as inconsistent with an investment-only intent and may require a notification to the FTC.

—Nomination of a candidate for the board of directors.

—Proposing corporate action requiring shareholders' approval.

—Soliciting proxies.

—Having a controlling shareholder, director, officer, or employee of the investor serve as a director of the company in which they have invested.

Unrelated business tax. If an institutional investor actively engages in providing direction to a company in which it owns stock, the action may be interpreted as entering the business. As a result, tax-exempt pension funds may have to pay tax paid by active investors.

Employee Retirement Income Security Act (ERISA). Current interpretation of the prudent man rule on pension fund managers requires holding a widely diversified portfolio. This tends to discourage investment in fewer kinds of equities with more active involvement in the management of the companies in the portfolio. Sometimes, pension managers interpreted their fiduciary responsibility as being their responsibility to sell their shares to corporate raiders who offered them a premium.

SEC rule 14a-8 (proxy rule). If ten or more shareholders discuss any issues that may result in a proxy vote, they must file all the communications of the discussion with the SEC. (This rule was relaxed in 1992.)

Executive disapproval. Chief executives often do not want their pension fund managers to challenge management of other companies.

Increasing popularity of indexed funds. Indexed investors have little incentive to participate in corporate governance. The California Public Employees Retirement System (CalPERS) is one of the exceptional indexed investors, however, that is active in monitoring management. Strictly indexed investors neither sell shares of badly performing companies nor buy shares of growing companies.

Takeover defense measures. Many of the takeover defense measures adopted by companies in the 1980s (see the appendix) have made it difficult for shareholders to make management accountable.

SEC rule 10b-5 (insider trading rule). Court rulings generally indicate that directors, officers, and other persons related to a corporation are prohibited from trading securities based on important information they have about the corporation that is not available to the public. Because the penalty for violating the rule is very severe, investors are strongly discouraged from communicating with the management closely if they want to trade securities of the company in the near future.

Source: Jacobs (1991, pp. 48–50, 83–97).

Table 2-5. *Ownership Concentration in Large Nonfinancial Corporations, Four Countries, 1970s–90*[a]

| Country | Ownership concentration | | |
	Mean	Median	Standard deviation
United States	25.4	20.9	16.0
United Kingdom	20.9	15.1	16.0
Japan	33.1	29.7	13.8
Germany	41.5	37.0	14.5

Source: Prowse (1994, table 9).

a. Samples are United States, 457 nonfinancial corporations in 1980; Japan, 143 mining and manufacturing corporations in 1984; Germany, 41 nonfinancial corporations in 1990; and United Kingdom, 85 manufacturing corporations in 1970.

banks or core manufacturing companies are common. In Germany large blocks of shares of many companies are often held by other companies or financial institutions, although cross-shareholdings are rare. Thus most shares of Japanese and German companies are held either by other industrial companies or by banks and insurance companies that have long-term relationships with them.[22] These shareholders are mainly interested in long-term performance of the companies they own and in developing transactions. The ownership of shares is also more concentrated in Germany and Japan than in the United States and the United Kingdom (table 2-5).

The distribution of categories of the largest shareholders of major U.S. and Japanese companies also differs. Although 72 percent of U.S. firms have institutional investors as the top shareholders, 66 percent of Japanese firms have either financial institutions with which they have a business relationship or parent or group (*keiretsu*) companies as their largest shareholders (table 2-6). More than 90 percent of Japanese companies believe that most of their owners are stable shareholders (table 2-7). Often these share-

22. Most Japanese companies have close transactional relationships with a bank (or a few banks). This bank is usually called the main bank of the company concerned, and often holds a significant equity stake in the company, has made large loans to it, and sometimes sends a director to its board. At the end of July 1993 banks collectively sent 1,556 directors and 509 auditors to 2,131 listed companies with a total of 39,882 directors and auditors. Kishida (1994, p. 209).

Table 2-6. *Distribution of Largest Shareholders in U.S. and Japanese Companies, by Category, 1988*

Percent

Category	U.S. companies	Japanese companies
Institutional investors	71.7	12.9
Financial institutions with business relationships	1.9	35.6
Nonfinancial companies with business relationships	1.9	9.4
Parent companies or companies in the same group (*keiretsu*)	1.9	30.7
Owner families	15.1	5.4
General investors	5.7	2.5
Other	1.9	3.5

Source: Kigyo Kodo ni Kansuru Chosa Kenkyu Iinkai (1988, p. 20). Data are from responses to a questionnaire sent to large manufacturing companies in Japan and the United States.

Table 2-7. *Prevalence of Stable Shareholders and Interlocking Shareholdings in Japanese Companies, 1990*

Stable shareholders as percent of all shareholders	Percent of responses[a]	Mutual shareholdings as percent of all shares issued	Percent of responses[b]
10	0.8	0	8.0
20	0.8	1–5	11.5
30	2.0	5–10	10.2
40	4.9	10–20	17.8
50	17.3	20–30	16.1
60	32.7	30–40	17.6
70	30.8	40–50	9.3
Other	10.6	50–60	6.6
		More than 60	2.9

Source: Shoji Homu Kenkyu Kai, "Kabushiki Kaishime, Antei Kabunushi ni Taisuru Jittai Chosa," conducted in February 1990, quoted in Economic Planning Agency of the Japanese Government (1992, pp. 232, 242).

a. Based on 490 responses.

b. Based on 410 responses.

holding relationships are mutual: some shareholders intentionally hold each other's shares as a protection against unwelcome take-over attempts or green-mailing.[23] Although cross-shareholdings are small on a bilateral basis, in the aggregate they are substantial.[24]

In Germany, more than half the shares of many companies are held by the parent companies and only a small percentage is traded on the stock market.[25] The nonfinancial business sector conse-quently holds almost 40 percent of the listed shares of German companies. Financial institutions are also important shareholders; banks hold 9 percent and insurance companies 11 percent of all domestically listed shares of German companies. German banks also act as custodians of investors' bearer shares (about 40 percent of the total market value of outstanding domestic shares was deposited in German banks at the end of 1988) and under certain rules can vote shares held in deposit on behalf of the depositors.[26] As a result, nearly one-half of listed corporate shares are under the control of German banks. The three largest banks collectively sent their representatives to the supervisory boards of sixty-six of the one hundred largest German companies in 1986.[27]

The participation of U.S. banks in corporate governance is slight in contrast with Japanese and German banks. U.S. banks can hold up to 5 percent of voting shares of nonfinancial companies through bank holding companies, which is essentially the same limit Japanese banks can hold, but they are discouraged from doing so by monetary authorities and unfavorable bankruptcy procedures for the banks with equity stakes (see the appendix). In fact, they have only 0.3 percent of total outstanding shares (table 2-4). When U.S. banks hold loans to a company and also own shares in it, the loan may be subordinated in relation to other

23. See the appendix for a summary on regulations of interlocking shareholdings. Green-mailing is carried out by a holder of a large block of a company's equity who pressures the company to buy back his shares at a premium over the current market price by threatening an unwanted takeover.

24. See Kester (1991, pp. 53–81) for a study of cross-shareholdings in the Mitsubishi group.

25. Schneider-Lenne (1992, p. 14).

26. Kester (1992). Regarding the regulations on the voting rights associated with the custody of bearer shares, see the appendix.

27. Aizawa (1989, p. 114).

creditors if the company fails. Bank regulators have also discouraged banks from taking control of nonfinancial companies for fear that condoning such control would encourage demands to allow nonfinancial companies to control banks.[28]

Acquisitions

Takeovers have been fairly common in the United States and the United Kingdom and are often regarded as a central function of stock markets. Through a takeover, a bidder who is prepared to pay more for the stock of a company than the prevailing market price can obtain the control of the company. Thus some observers believe takeovers facilitate the transfer of control of a company from inefficient to efficient management. Even the threat of a takeover alerts a management to do its best to maximize the market value of its company.[29]

In Japan and Germany stock markets are much less important as means of acquiring control of corporations. Takeovers are not considered necessary to encourage efficient management: direct interaction between large shareholders and management plays a more important role in rectifying managerial problems. Although voluntary mergers (either for strategic reasons or for rescuing weakened companies) are common, hostile takeovers have been virtually nonexistent.[30] Rules on market acquisitions in Japan and Germany are generally no more restrictive than in the United States and the United Kingdom.[31] But for institutional reasons,

28. This explanation is based on conversations with economists of the U.S. Federal Reserve Board.

29. Franks and Mayer (1990, p. 191).

30. Flick Brothers' acquisition of Feldmuehle Nobel in 1989 is the first example of a hostile acquisition in Germany (Franks and Mayer, 1990, pp. 228–29). In Japan, there have been several attempts at hostile takeovers or green-mailing, but no clear-cut cases of successful takeovers have been reported (Kishida, 1994, pp. 407–09).

31. See the appendix. Franks and Mayer (1990, p. 229) and Schneider-Lenne (1992, p. 22) observed that takeover rules in Germany are less strict than those in the United Kingdom. Kester (1991), who conducted very detailed field research on Japanese mergers and acquisitions, has commented, "it is difficult to conclude that either the spirit or the letter of Japanese law is fundamentally more inimical to mergers and acquisitions than is, say, American or British law. . . . It seems unlikely that even administrative guidance regarding domestic mergers and acquisitions in Japan will emerge as a severe impediment to Japanese combinations, if in fact, it was in the first place" (pp. 102–03).

including stable shareholding (Germany and Japan), shareholder voting rules (Germany), and strong labor participation in supervisory boards (Germany), hostile takeovers are much more difficult to conclude successfully.

Many economists have observed that the American and British type of corporate governance that combines the unstable ownership of shares with takeovers as a central mechanism to discipline underperforming management is by no means an ideal system.[32] Although the system does have some advantages, Japanese and German corporate governance systems have others. Takeovers are necessary in the United States and the United Kingdom, they maintain, because of the absence of active owner-investors, such as banks, that can rectify the mismanagement of a firm without disruptive and costly takeovers. In Japan and Germany, takeovers are far less necessary because large shareholders can interact directly with management.

Reflecting these institutional differences are the countermeasures against takeover threats. U.S. companies can deploy the most impressive array of means against hostile takeovers (see the appendix). Some of the most potent, such as the poison pill defense, can be used by the management without asking shareholders. Many of these measures are either illegal (share repurchase) or cannot be used without obtaining shareholders' approval (the golden parachute, the poison pill) in Japan.[33]

One instrument of U.S. takeover defense that requires special attention is changing a state's corporate law by lobbying the state legislature. Although the management and the employees of a company have a very strong interest in the state laws on takeovers, the shareholders of the company are often spread all over the United States and have little leverage in the state concerned. As a result, the political balance of power favors the entrenched management. Because of this, more than

32. See Porter (1992); Kester (1991, 1992); Jacobs (1991); Prowse (1990); and Franks and Mayer (1990).

33. A golden parachute is a provision in the employment contract of top executives guaranteeing a large compensation in case they lose their jobs following a successful takeover.

forty states have made hostile takeovers much more difficult to achieve.[34]

If a company's management can significantly influence state corporate laws, it is in effect changing its corporate charter without asking shareholders, which is unthinkable in other countries. However, as international equity investment increases, the relative balance of political power between management and shareholders in other countries will become more like it is in the United States. The shareholders will be spread thinly across countries, but the interest of the management and the employees will be concentrated in one country. This imbalance is likely to become important for the European Union, where financial markets are being progressively integrated.

Paid-In Capital and Accounting Rules

There are significant differences in the ways countries write rules on the use of paid-in capital, the amount paid in by shareholders, including the premium over the face value of shares (see the appendix). In the United States, legal restrictions on cash distributions to shareholders (such as dividend payouts) other than from current or accumulated profits are very weak. In most U.S. states, companies do not have to allocate all paid-in capital to the stated capital; and they can keep the remainder as the capital surplus. This surplus is available for future dividends. Even when the net assets fall short of the stated capital, companies in many states can still pay a dividend from the profits of the past two years (the so-called nimble dividend). It is thus usually possible for the board of directors to pay out dividends or to buy its company's shares by reducing the paid-in capital unless the company faces imminent insolvency.[35]

---

34. Roe (1993), Easterbrook and Fischel (1991), and Jacobs (1991) claim that the U.S. federal system, which allows fifty states and the District of Columbia to legislate corporate laws, itself favors management at the expense of shareholders. Romano (1993) provides a counterargument.

35. In the United States, creditors often use bond covenants to protect their interests. Most unsecured bonds issued by the companies with credit ratings between AAA and AA carry a clause that prohibits the company from providing collateral (the so-called negative

In Japan, Germany, and France the cash distribution to shareholders from the paid-in capital is restricted by law and requires the consent of all the creditors. Companies cannot pay dividends or buy back their own shares unless their net worth exceeds the amount of paid-in capital so as to keep paid-in capital for creditors' security. Companies in these countries also have to retain part of the profits as added security for creditors. The restrictions on distributions to shareholders were weak in the United Kingdom until 1980, but they are now more in line with those of Japan, France, and Germany (see the appendix).

There are also differences in accounting rules. In the United States and United Kingdom accounting rules are oriented toward providing economic information to shareholders; the protection of other stakeholders, including suppliers and employees, is a lesser objective. Marketable securities are usually evaluated at market prices rather than historical prices. Tax rules have relatively little influence on accounting rules. In the other three countries, most marketable securities are evaluated at historical prices or the lower of historical or market prices. Real estate is also evaluated at historical prices. Because equity and real estate prices have risen considerably over the years, these accounting rules have protected stakeholders, including suppliers and employees, by conservatively measuring the net assets of a company and restricting dividend payouts. Tax rules strongly influence accounting rules. Reflecting these differences, the reported earnings of Continental companies are generally more conservatively evaluated than those of British companies and, to a lesser degree, those of U.S. companies. On an index on which earnings of U.S. companies are set at 100, for instance, earnings of U.K. companies would be 125 and those of Continental companies would be considerably lower—France, 97; Netherlands, 91; Belgium, 88; Germany, 87; and Spain 85.[36]

---

pledge clause) for other debts. However, for these companies, clauses on dividend restrictions are rarely imposed.

36. S. J. Gray, quoted in Tzamouranis and others (1993). The figures are estimated by using audited U.S. generally accepted accounting principles (GAAP) reconciliations of earnings of large non-U.S. companies listed on the New York Stock Exchange. The differences are probably understated because some of the companies used for the study had

Bankruptcy Procedures

Bankruptcy procedures impose hard budget constraints on limited liability companies in modern economies. The primary purpose of bankruptcy law for such companies is to provide a legal framework to resolve conflicts among various classes of creditors (secured creditors, unsecured creditors, unpaid employees, and so on) and equity holders in an orderly and fair manner when a company no longer performs its contractual obligations. Usually, bankruptcy laws have two sets of procedures: liquidation and reorganization (rehabilitation). When a company is deemed no longer viable, it is liquidated and the recovered assets are distributed among creditors following contractual priority (the absolute priority rule) under the supervision of a bankruptcy court. If there are remaining assets, which is unlikely, equity holders can be reimbursed. When the prospects for creditors, including employees and other stakeholders, are deemed better if the company concerned is allowed to operate with some debt relief rather than if it is liquidated, the reorganization procedure is carried out under the supervision of a bankruptcy court. Under this procedure the absolute priority rule is sometimes overridden to allow the firm to operate.

U.S. bankruptcy law covers both liquidation and reorganization, but it emphasizes reorganization. Compared with the laws of other countries, U.S. law puts more weight on protecting the debtor than it does the creditor. Under the rehabilitation process (chapter 11 of the bankruptcy code), the management of the failed company usually retains control and has the power normally granted to court-appointed administrators in other countries. The contractual order of priority among creditors and shareholders is often

---

already adjusted their domestic reports to U.S. practice to some degree. When Daimler-Benz became the first German company to be fully listed on the New York Stock Exchange in September 1993, it reported two sets of profit figures. In the first half of the year, the company lost DM 949 million under the U.S. generally accepted accounting principles but reported a profit of DM 168 million under German accounting rules ("Germany Seeks U.S. Concession on Listings," *Financial Times*, September 27, 1993, p. 21). This example indicates that, although German rules may be more conservative than U.S. rules on average, they seem to allow companies to smooth out their profits and may give an upward bias to profit figures during cyclical downturns.

violated because of the complicated structure of the approval process of the reorganization plan. Consequently, the protection of collateral is not very strong; sometimes chapter 11 proceedings produce results biased toward managers, shareholders, and junior creditors of a failed company.[37]

Japan also has liquidation and reorganization processes, but because the system is somewhat inflexible in practical applications and a formal court procedure of bankruptcy can be costly, private arrangements among creditors of a failing company and arrangements involving banks are preferred, especially for smaller companies.[38] These arrangements generally follow the broad outlines of a formal process. Secured creditors are strongly protected, but under one of the reorganization procedures (*kaisha kosei ho*), the protection of collateral is somewhat restricted to facilitate a company's rehabilitation.

German bankruptcy law provides for liquidation, but has no strong provisions for reorganization. The protection of collateral is very strong, so that rehabilitating a failed company under formal procedures is difficult. As in Japan, private arrangements between creditors and the management, often involving banks, are preferred to formal court processes. Major revisions of the bankruptcy laws are now under discussion.

The French bankruptcy law of 1985 strongly emphasizes rehabilitation through reorganization (such as the sale of the company) rather than liquidation in order to protect employment. Reflecting this emphasis, the creditors' position is relatively weak compared with that of the employees. The creditors, including secured creditors, are often forced to accept large reductions in the value of their claims. The management of a failed company may face strict sanctions.

Bankruptcy law in the United Kingdom provides for both liquidation and reorganization. The protection of collateral is strong, sometimes making rehabilitation of a failed company difficult under formal procedures. Strict sanctions are imposed against the directors of failed companies.

---

37. See Jensen (1991) and Franks and Torous (1992) for discussions of this problem.

38. See Sheard (1994) for an extensive review on the involvement of main banks in corporate restructuring.

To sum up, in the United States the position of the management and shareholders during a bankruptcy is favored at the expense of creditors. In France, employees are favored at the expense of creditors. In Germany, the United Kingdom, and to a lesser extent Japan, the departure from the absolute priority rule is slight, and the creditors, especially secured creditors, are relatively well protected, which may contribute to a lower cost of debt. But a viable company may face premature dissolution under formal bankruptcy procedures.

Conclusions

Corporate control practices and laws in the five countries represent two philosophies. In the United States and the United Kingdom, control relies more on selling a company to the highest bidder to improve performance. Although shareholders' voting power and the transferability of shares are less restricted in these two countries, there are more restrictions on the issues that can be decided by shareholders. In Japan, Germany, and France, control relies more on the direct interaction between shareholders and management, with binding voting power on the part of shareholders. Corporate structures are less stable in the United States and the United Kingdom than in Japan and Germany. Stock markets provide the market for corporate control in the United States and the United Kingdom, but not in Japan and Germany.

The United States and United Kingdom pose a number of impediments for even relatively large shareholders (those who own several percent or more of a company's shares) who might wish to change the behavior of management directly. Information is usually limited to publicly disclosed materials, and the acquisition of inside information is strongly discouraged. Shareholders' direct interaction with management is also discouraged by regulations on communications among shareholders, the generally restrictive shareholder proposal system, and the broad interpretation of the business judgment rule. Even large shareholders thus have difficulty in giving binding instructions to management. One manifestation of this weak control is the exorbitant executive compensation in many large U.S. and British companies. What most shareholders can do is to sell their shares to someone who is ready to amass enough shares to take over management of the company. Even this control mechanism is restricted by state antitakeover measures in the United States.

Recognizing these problems, some U.S. institutional investors have become more active shareholders. Such public pension funds as the California Public Employees Retirement System and the New York City Employees' Retirement System have begun to communicate directly with management to improve the performance of the companies whose stocks they hold.[39] They have demanded increases in the number of outside independent directors on company boards, the separation of the roles of the chairman of the board and the chief executive officer to improve the monitoring function of boards, and the formation of compensation, nomination (for new directors), and audit committees that consist of independent directors. Insurance companies and corporate pension funds have been less active in these matters because they do not want to offend companies with which they do business. In the United Kingdom the Cadbury Committee produced a report in 1992 to rectify problems of corporate governance. The report recommended changes in the board structure broadly similar to those demanded by U.S. public pension funds.[40]

Although these ideas point in the right direction, some critics contend that the appointment of more independent directors is not an effective solution to governance problems because too often the outsiders have a cozy relationship with the executive directors and are involved with their duties only a few days a month.[41] The critics recommend that shareholders be given stronger voting power and be more directly involved in monitoring and auditing management.

As for hostile takeovers or threats of takeover as a way to discipline corporate management, they do seem to work, but large

39. David Vise, "Calif. Pension Fund Plans an Investment in Power," *Washington Post*, November 11, 1993, p. H1.

40. Peter Martin, "Taming the Overmighty Boss," *Financial Times*, December 2, 1992, p. 20.

41. See Jacobs (1991, chap. 8); and Sheridan and Kendall (1992, chap. 5).

shareholders (or large banks that control proxy votes) should be able to monitor poorly performing companies more closely and force them to change strategy or replace the management. For this power to work well, however, large shareholders must have access to detailed information about their firms, and regulations on insider trading, although indispensable to protect small shareholders from abuses by large shareholders, make it difficult to monitor and control management. The vague definition of insider trading rules in the United States and the severe penalties against violations are strong deterrents to effective communication between large shareholders and management.

For example, a company cannot include detailed information on research and development or investment projects in publicly disclosed documents because it would not wish to reveal such information to its competitors. The costs of intangible investment, such as training for employees, are also difficult to explain to shareholders. As a result, investors tend to concentrate on the bottom line of quarterly reports. Because most of the R&D and training expenditures will not bear fruit immediately, they are often treated as a drag on profits. By initiating a hostile takeover of a company with large intangible investments and cutting back these apparently unprofitable activities, a new management can report better profits—at least temporarily—to shareholders. The management and the employees of companies facing possible takeover will be discouraged from making long-term commitments because it would be too risky.

In Japan, Germany, and France, large shareholders can communicate discreetly with management and can influence company performance because they can always use their voting power to nominate their candidate to a company's board and express their opinions on its management to the board of directors (or supervisory board in Germany). In Japan a shareholders' meeting often lasts less than one hour, which has been interpreted as indicating the weak position of shareholders in Japanese companies.[42] But large shareholders in Japan do not have to communicate with the

---

42. See Kishida (1991, chap. 2).

management at shareholders meetings. Instead, they can, and do, discuss with the management any item on the agenda, including proposed new members for the board of directors, well before the meeting. Because laws against insider trading are explicit, large shareholders do not have to fear close communication with management. After such private discussions, the shareholders can simply give their consenting proxy to the management. As a result, management usually has the majority vote at the shareholders' meeting.

In Germany, Japan, and France management is better protected from hostile takeovers than it is in the United States. Extensive cross-shareholding among Japanese companies, including financial institutions, makes it very difficult to succeed in a hostile takeover. In Germany, too, takeovers are hard to engineer. Large banks can exercise proxy votes of stocks in their custody accounts. Often they control a large block of votes without holding many shares themselves. And company employees have the right to elect from one-third to one-half the members on the powerful supervisory boards, which also discourages takeover attempts. In both France and Germany, corporate shareholdings of other companies are permitted and common. The French government was also a substantial shareholder in French corporations until the privatization of important nationalized companies by conservative governments in the past decade. This, too, made it difficult to take control of these firms through the stock market until recently. Finally, for hostile takeovers to succeed, the new management sometimes must dispose of a large part of the assets of the company and dismiss many employees. But in Japan, France, and Germany it is difficult to lay off workers of a firm that is not on the verge of collapse. The management and the employees have long-term implicit contracts of job security, and they must be honored. Long-term investments, employee training, and R&D activities can thus be carried out in a more secure environment.

Chapter 3

Corporate Governance, Corporate Objectives, and Company Performance

*T*HIS chapter develops a model that explains some of the important behavioral differences between companies in the United States and United Kingdom and those in Japan and Germany. The model focuses on the order of importance of various stakeholders (creditors, top executives, core employees, and shareholders) and discusses the comparative advantages of two governance structures in relation to the cost of capital and the use of labor.[1]

A Theoretical Framework

Because of differences in the structure of corporate governance, corporations in different countries have advantages and disadvantages in their capacity to engage in various business activities. The following list indicates some of the important elements of this capacity.

—How well are creditors protected in case of bankruptcy? The cost of debt is higher in countries with weak protection.

—How strong is the power of shareholders to intervene in the management of the company? The cost of equity capital depends on the power of control associated with the equity.

1. In the following analysis I have tried to synthesize evidence on the behavioral differences of companies across countries. But most of the literature compares U.S. and Japanese companies. Therefore any conclusions I derive for the companies in Germany, France, and the United Kingdom have more speculative elements than do conclusions for the United States and Japan.

—How credible are the commitments management gives to employees? If management cannot ensure the continuity of commitment beyond its own tenure, employees will not invest their time and effort to acquire firm-specific skills, even if management gives a commitment to hire them indefinitely. Employees would prefer to acquire more widely marketable skills to improve their chances of being hired by other companies.[2]

—How credible are the commitments management gives to suppliers or distributors to continue relations in the future? If the commitments are not credible, suppliers and distributors will not invest in the capital equipment specific to the transactions with the company in question. Vertical integration of suppliers may help ensure inputs, but running a large vertically integrated company involves other costs and difficulties.[3]

—How quickly and easily can a company return capital to investors? How quickly and easily can it lay off or terminate employees? If changes in the business environment occur very quickly, a company must be able to adapt quickly and cheaply.

The relative importance of the stakeholders (creditors, top executives, core employees, and shareholders) to corporate assets is the key to understanding the performance of companies incorporated in different countries. In principle, this relationship is independent of a firm's profit maximization. Management can always get the greatest possible profit for shareholders under the contractual constraints of this relationship. For example, results of a questionnaire sent to large U.S. and Japanese companies asking them to list their most important management objectives have shown that both U.S. and Japanese companies, in similar magnitudes, put primary emphasis on profit maximization (table 3-1). But the relative importance of the various stakeholders of the company can vary widely from country to country.

2. It is possible to write an explicit employment contract asking employees to acquire company-specific skills in exchange for permanent employment. But it would be very difficult to enforce this kind of contract and could allow employees to shirk their duties.

3. Williamson (1985, chaps. 3–5) discusses governance structures of large manufacturing operations.

Table 3-1. *Most Important Management Objectives of Large U.S. and Japanese Companies, 1988*
Percent

Objectives	U.S. companies	Japanese companies	Objectives	U.S. companies	Japanese companies
Profit maximization	53.6	45.0	Diversification of business	3.6	9.4
Increasing market share	17.9	12.4	Increasing dividend	0	0
Sales maximization	3.6	5.4	Stable employment	0	1.5
Improvement of technology	19.6	16.8	Improvement in public perception	0	0.5
Internationalization of business	0	7.4	Others	1.8	1.5

Source: Kigyo Kodo ni Kansuru Chosa Kenkyu Iinkai (1988, p. 2). The table is based on a questionnaire sent to large manufacturing companies in Japan and the United States.

For large companies whose stocks are traded publicly, the hypothesized hierarchical importance of the various factors is as follows:

Relationship A: Japan and Germany
   Creditors > a large number of core employees > top executives > shareholders (strictly defined earned profit) > other employees

Relationship B: United States
   Top executives > creditors > a very small number of core employees > shareholders (liberally defined earned profit plus a part of paid-in capital) > a large number of other employees

Important differences between the two sequences are the positions of core employees and top executives. In addition, U.S. shareholders have a larger claim, before employees in a junior position, than do Japanese and German shareholders.

   These relationships depend not only on laws and regulations, but also on implicit contracts, supported by customs and court rulings, between management and employees. In Relationship A the first inequality is imposed by the bankruptcy laws in Japan and Germany that respect the absolute priority of creditors over the other stakeholders. The second and third inequalities come from the implicit contract of semipermanent employment between management and core employees and the relatively strict control of executive compensation by shareholders. The shareholders' rights to distribution are strictly regulated by the corporate laws of Japan and Germany. The last inequality shows that there are a number of non-core part-time or temporary workers in Japanese companies.

In Relationship B the first inequality is caused by chapter 11 of the U.S. bankruptcy code, which is extremely lenient to the management, and shareholders' weak control over executive compensation. The second inequality arises because any large company has a critical core of workers for its smooth operation, and they cannot be released unless the company is liquidated. The shareholders' claim is more important than it is in Japan or Germany because of differences in corporate law and accounting rules. The last inequality is caused by the situation that most employees in the United States are not protected by implicit contracts guaranteeing permanent employment. They can be laid off at short notice.

These hierarchical relationships can be understood more easily by considering what happens to Japanese and U.S. companies facing severe financial difficulties. When a large Japanese company faces difficulties, it begins cutting part-time and temporary workers and the overtime of regular workers. Then it reduces stock dividends and executive compensation. In the meantime the company tries to maintain core workers by shifting them among factories and branches. As long as the company has undistributed profits, it will not lay off regular workers because of current losses. It will rely on natural attrition and more attractive early retirement packages. If its financial position continues to deteriorate, it will cut regular workers after consulting with its union. When the company faces a real danger of bankruptcy, its main bank joins the management and the bank sends a director or directors to the failing company.

The sequence is very different for a typical large U.S. company. Even if the company is still making money, it may lay off regular workers to improve its balance sheet. A company that is losing money may continue to pay dividends from its paid-in capital. When the company faces a real danger of bankruptcy, it will apply for chapter 11 relief. The current managers will retain control for a considerable time.

The Commitment to Permanent Employment

In Japan and Germany the employment of core workers is fairly secure because of implicit contracts between management and labor.[4] This commitment is credible for various reasons. First, management is organized to be very stable. It can maintain continuity owing to this stability. Second, major shareholders put more emphasis on long-term growth and the viability of the company than on short-term financial gains. Important shareholders of Japanese and German companies have transactions with the companies they hold, and they have a vital interest in the continuation of this relationship. This emphasis contrasts sharply with demands made by U.S. shareholders: 80 percent of U.S. shareholders want share prices to increase rapidly; 80 percent of Japanese shareholders find either the growth or stability of the business more important (table 3-2). Finally, paid-in capital and undistributed profits provide greater security for core employees in Japan and Germany than they can do in the United States.

In the United States, even if management makes a commitment to hire workers for long periods, the commitment is usually less credible than it is in Japan and Germany.[5] The turnover among top

4. In Japan there are no explicit lifetime employment contracts between management and employees. In fact, the Japanese civil codes prohibit employment contracts longer than five years and the Labor Standard Law generally prohibits contracts longer than one year. Legally, so-called lifetime employment means a contract of indefinite duration. Management can, in principle, lay off workers with one month's notification. But because of court rulings on layoffs, employers who lay off workers for economic reasons are required to observe the following procedures. The employers must prove that it is necessary to lay off workers, must have tried to avoid layoffs by reallocating workers, must show objective criteria regarding who is laid off, and must negotiate with the relevant labor unions. The labor unions' strong opposition to layoffs also discourages companies from releasing workers. Finally, the Japanese employment insurance system provides financial assistance to companies facing difficulties to keep on temporarily idle workers. See Koshiro (1989).

5. There are, of course, important exceptions. Until recently, IBM was well known for its lifetime employment policy. And although it has started to lay off workers, IBM has been providing a very generous severance package that mitigates its breach of the implicit contract.

Table 3-2. *Most Important Concerns of Shareholders According to Management of Large U.S. and Japanese Companies, 1988*
Percent

Concern	U.S. companies	Japanese companies
Increasing dividend	3.8	6.0
Raising share prices	79.2	12.1
Growth of business	14.8	56.4
Stability of business	3.8	24.0
Fulfillment of social responsibilities	0	2.0

Source: Kigyo Kodo ni Kansuru Chosa Kenkyu Iinkai (1988, p. 21). The table is based on a questionnaire sent to large manufacturing companies in Japan and the United States.

management is high, and managers are often appointed by outsiders to the company after takeovers. As a result, the continuity of the employment policy cannot be ensured.[6] Long-term employment is also compromised because shareholders are more interested in short-term financial gains than in the growth and the stability of the business. Finally, shareholders' paid-in capital is less committed to the business institutionally.

Reflecting these differences in commitment are differences in the reactions of companies facing financial difficulties. The most likely method both U.S. and Japanese companies use to overcome the deterioration of business is to reduce costs other than labor, although 50 percent more Japanese companies choose this method first (table 3-3). U.S. companies rely more on cutting labor costs and eliminating unprofitable lines of business.[7] Four percent of Japanese companies chose reducing executive compensation as the most likely, compared to 1.8 percent of U.S. companies. Because executive compensation is a small part of total costs, reducing it cannot be very important to fighting a financial crisis. But as the

6. For an expanded explanation of this problem, see Shleifer and Summers (1988).

7. Labor relations law in Japan makes it very difficult for a company to have a U.S.-style layoff agreement with its union. Any group of workers can form a new union in Japan, and the company is obliged to consult with the union when the company wants to lay off workers in that union. In the United States a union that obtains a majority of votes represents all the workers in a plant. Even if a Japanese company makes a seniority-based layoff agreement with the current union, young workers may withdraw and establish a new union.

Table 3-3. *Most Likely Means to Overcome Deterioration of Business,*
U.S. and Japanese Companies, 1988
Percent

Method	U.S. companies	Japanese companies
Reduce costs other than labor	55.4	75.7
Eliminate unprofitable lines of business	21.4	2.0
Reduce labor cost	17.9	4.5
Reduce executive compensation	1.8	4.0
Reduce business equipment investment	1.8	4.5
Use reserves	1.8	5.9
Reduce dividend	0	2.5
Reduce welfare benefits for employees	0	0.5
Reduce R&D investment	0	0

Source: Kigyo Kodo ni Kansuru Chosa Kenkyu Iinkai (1988, p. 4). The table is based on a questionnaire sent to large manufacturing companies in Japan and the United States.

second most likely means to overcome the problem, 9.9 percent of Japanese companies chose this means; no U.S. companies chose it.

Methods of reducing labor costs are also very different in the two countries. Natural attrition is chosen by one-third of companies in both, but although outright layoffs are very important to 29 percent of U.S. companies, less than 2 percent of Japanese companies consider this the most important means (table 3-4). Japanese companies rely on reducing overtime and on seconding employees to other companies.

U.S. companies adjust their labor forces mostly by changing the number of employees; Japanese companies rely more on adjusting working hours (table 3-5). Moreover, in Japan the variability of labor input is less than one-half of the variability of production, indicating either labor hoarding or secondment of workers from production to other assignments. In the United States the variability of labor input is more in line with that of production. The pattern of adjustment for German companies is closer to that of U.S. companies. Because this observation is contrary to the anecdotal evidence that German companies try to maintain stable employment by shortening working hours, further analysis is necessary.

Table 3-4. *Preferred Means of Cutting Labor Costs, U.S. and Japanese Companies, 1988*
Percent

Means	U.S. companies	Japanese companies
Layoffs	29.1	1.8
Natural attrition	32.7	37.7
Reduction of overtime	20.0	44.9
Stopping wage and salary increases	1.8	2.4
Rotating excess employees	7.3	5.4
Seconding workers to other companies	0	7.8
Eliminating posts	9.1	0

Source: Kigyo Kodo ni Kansuru Chosa Kenkyu Iinkai (1988, p. 5). The table is based on a questionnaire sent to large manufacturing companies in Japan and the United States.

Table 3-5. *Standard Deviation of Changes in Manufacturing Production, Employees, Working Hours, and Labor Input, United States, Japan, and Germany, 1961–69, 1970–79, 1980–91*

Type of change	1961–69	1970–79	1980–91
United States			
Production	4.22	7.02	4.76
Employees	2.71	4.71	3.39
Working hours	1.21	1.56	1.51
Labor input[a]	3.36	5.74	4.37
Japan			
Production	6.42	8.39	3.88
Employees	3.41	2.35	1.11
Working hours	1.30	2.40	1.24
Labor input[a]	2.97	3.22	1.24
Germany			
Production	5.32	4.95	3.65
Employees	3.33	3.53	2.38
Working hours	1.93	1.78	1.11
Labor input[a]	4.83	4.49	2.63

Source: Keizai Kikaku Cho (1992, p. 261).

a. Employees × working hours.

Executive Compensation

In the United States and to a lesser extent the United Kingdom, executive compensation is not under the effective control of a corporation's owners. Even after a successful hostile takeover, the outgoing top managers can receive large severance packages without the shareholders' approval. And, in the United States, management can continue to control the company even after a bankruptcy. Executive compensation in the United States is thus one of the most secure claims to the assets of the company. When a Japanese company faces financial difficulties, however, executive compensation and upper-management salaries are usually reduced before labor costs are cut. In German companies employee representation on supervisory boards puts some restraint on the remuneration of the executives, as does the requirement that shareholders approve compensation.[8]

This very secure position of top managers in U.S. companies, compared with the unstable job security of most workers, makes it difficult to generate a sense of corporate loyalty among lower-level employees. The Japanese practice of promoting employees to boards of directors, the German system of employee participation on the supervisory board, and the more effective control of executive compensation in Japan and Germany help create the sense of a unified corporate community among top managers and a large number of core employees.[9]

Governance, Capital, and Labor

Some aspects of the governance structures of Japanese and German companies, including their close relationship with banks

8. Sheridan and Kendall (1992, p. 103).

9. The importance of commitment by both management and labor in implementing the efficient lean production system, first developed by Toyota, is emphasized by Womack, Jones, and Roos (1990, pp. 248–49). "The problem with the American pattern is that it is extremely corrosive to the vital personal relationships at the core of any production process. . . . The consequence is a distinct lack of commitment on the part of workers and suppliers. . . . Lean production, by contrast, is inherently a system of reciprocal obligation. Workers share a fate with their employer, suppliers share a fate with the assembler. When the system works properly, it generates a willingness to participate actively and to initiate the continuous improvements that are at the very heart of leanness."

and the strong voting power of shareholders, seem to give them some advantage over U.S. or British companies in gaining access to low-cost capital. Japanese companies also seem to have an advantage in realizing the lean production system in manufacturing because of their maintenance of long-term employment and their long-term relations with suppliers. However, the same long-term relations may generate inefficiency in the distribution system by limiting competition.

Governance and the Cost of Capital

Differences among countries in the cost of capital have received considerable attention as important factors determining the international competitiveness of industries, the level of investment, the direction of foreign direct investment flows, and productivity growth rates. The cost of capital is defined as the minimum pretax real rate of return that an investment project must earn to make the project attractive to investors. Because the cost of capital determines the discount factor, which is used to evaluate the cash flow from investment projects, it affects the time horizon of a company; the higher the cost of capital, the higher the discount rate.

The cost of capital is determined by the cost of debt, the cost of equity, the financial structure (leverage) of the company, and the tax system.[10] The cost of debt is the real cost of net debt after taking account of the deductibility of interest payments from taxable corporate income. The cost of debt is determined by the real cost of default-free debt and the default risk premium. The cost of equity is the real cost of raising equity capital from the viewpoint of the management of the company or shareholders.[11] The weighted average of the cost of debt and the cost of equity deter-

10. See Fukao (1993, appendix) for a detailed discussion on various concepts of financing costs.

11. It is possible to distinguish the following two concepts related to equity finance: the expected return on the equity from the viewpoint of management with its inside information on the company, and the expected return on the equity from the viewpoint of shareholders who have bought the newly issued equity. These two returns can diverge. When the stock price of a company is overvalued in relation to the inside information of the management, the cost of equity finance for management is lower than for the expected return on

mines the cost of funds. The weights depend on the financial structure (leverage) of the firm. Finally, the cost of capital is derived from the cost of funds by taking account of the impact of the tax system on the company making an investment. Among the most important elements of the tax system are the corporate tax rate, the relationship between depreciation allowances under the corporate tax system and the economic rate of depreciation of the project to be financed, and any investment tax credits or investment grants.

The elements of the cost of capital are determined simultaneously by the interaction between the financial decisions of the company and market forces. The relative costs of debt and equity capital affect the leverage. At the same time, the leverage of the company affects the cost of debt through the default risk premium.

The increasing integration of financial markets tends to reduce international differences in financing costs of investment. International arbitrage transactions narrow the differences in nominal returns on default-free debts adjusted for expected changes in exchange rates. If future movements of exchange rates between two countries are expected to correspond to inflation rate differentials, real interest rates in the two countries will tend to converge.[12] A convergence of long-term real interest rates can be expected under highly integrated financial markets because exchange rates fluctuate around purchasing power parity in the long run. However, exchange rates often diverge from purchasing power parity

---

equity for new shareholders. Because the decision to issue new equity is usually taken by the management of a company with either the implicit or explicit consent of existing shareholders, only the equity financing that is advantageous for management and the existing shareholders will be implemented. In the rest of this section, I analyze the cost of equity finance from this viewpoint.

12. Because international transactions tend to narrow the differences in nominal returns on bonds adjusted for expected changes in exchange rates, the following equation tends to hold: $r_d = r_d^\star + x$, where r_d is currency A's interest rate, $r_d^\star$ is currency B's interest rate, and x is the expected rate of appreciation of currency B against currency A. If the future movements of exchange rates between two countries are expected to correspond to inflation rate differentials, the following equation results: $x = pi - pi^\star$, where pi is the expected inflation in country A and $pi^\star$ is the expected inflation in country B. If these two relationships hold, the real interest rates of the two countries will converge. From the previous equations, an equation showing equalization of real interest rates can be derived: $r_d - pi = r_d^\star - pi^\star$.

levels in the short run. Expected changes in exchange rates may therefore differ from expected inflation differentials, resulting in some real interest rate differentials across countries at the shorter end of the term structure.

Greater integration of financial markets also tends to reduce the international differences in the cost of equity. In a given national equity market, the cost of equity capital is determined by the opportunity cost of investing in equities, the degree of risk aversion on the part of investors, and the inherent risk in owning shares of a specific company based in the country. The globalization of financial markets reduces the real interest rate differential across countries, limiting the importance of the opportunity cost of investing in equities. International diversification of equity portfolios also works to reduce national differences in risk aversion by allowing residents of all countries to participate in foreign markets for equity, limiting the importance of investors' risk aversion. Although the third factor—the inherent risk of owning a company based in a country—is not influenced directly by international financial arbitrage, the other two factors tend to reduce the international difference in the cost of equity.

The cost of capital also depends on the amount of a firm's leverage—the relative importance of debt and equity in its financing. International differences in the extent of leverage depend on institutional factors related to financial structure that affect the degree of risk to creditors that is associated with high leverage. In financial transactions, creditors and borrowers do not have equal access to information, and conflicts of interest among creditors are often acute. When a company faces financial distress, these factors often make the renegotiation of financial claims difficult. For example, when a company has a large number of creditors, they are unlikely all to be well informed about the conditions of the company and may be less inclined to make financial concessions than they would be if there were fewer, better informed creditors.

For companies with strong relationships with banks, these problems are less severe. When a bank holds a large share of a firm's debt and equity and is well informed, it is well placed to judge whether to provide it with financial assistance.[13] Observers often contend that the main-bank system in Japan and the Hausbank system in Germany enjoy these advantages. Although monitoring by banks inevitably imposes limits on borrowers' freedom of action, and often implies higher effective borrowing costs, companies that have close relationships with banks often maintain a greater leverage without incurring undue risks of bankruptcy or financial distress.[14] They may be willing to pay slightly higher interest rates because the banks have a stake in providing support if that becomes necessary.[15]

Another factor likely to affect leverage is international differences in the bankruptcy law. The differences are unlikely to affect the risk of high-quality corporate bonds, but they make the riskiness of claims on less healthy companies dependent on the country in which they operate. More than in other countries, for example, bankruptcy law in the United States puts more importance on preserving the ability of debtors to continue operating than it does on protecting the claims of creditors. This is likely to raise the cost of debt for U.S. companies relative to that for other companies. Differences in sanctions against directors of failed businesses, which can affect the behavior of management in businesses facing financial difficulties, may also influence the relative riskiness of claims on businesses across countries.

Differences also exist across countries in restrictions on management's freedom to alter a company's financial structure. U.S. businesses are usually permitted to pay dividends or to retire shares with funds paid in by shareholders, for example, but Japanese and German firms are not permitted to do so in normal circumstances. Because U.S. companies have this freedom, their

---

13. Hoshi, Kashyap, and Scharfstein (1990b).

14. Prowse (1990) found that Japanese financial institutions often own a large amount of equity in those companies to which they lend, and the agency costs of issuing debt are mitigated to a greater extent in Japan than they are in the United States.

15. Hoshi, Kashyap, and Scharfstein (1990a) showed that investments by Japanese companies that have close relationships with their banks are less affected by their level of cash flow than are investments of other Japanese companies. And Hoshi, Kashyap, and Scharfstein (1990b) demonstrated that Japanese firms in industrial groups that have close financial relationships with their banks, suppliers, and customers tend to invest more and sell more after the onset of financial distress than do companies not in such groups.

credit ratings may deteriorate suddenly. This risk is likely to raise the cost of debt for U.S. companies relative to that of non-U.S. companies.

Macroeconomic stability and various institutional arrangements, including bank-business relationships, the risk of incurring large legal liability, bankruptcy procedures, and government policy regarding industry, affect the risk of investing in the equity of companies based in a given country. The strength of the rights of shareholders is significantly different across countries, and it affects the cost of equity. This is similar to the relationship between the bond covenants and the credit rating of the bond. "A stock that has little or no ownership rights involves greater risks, thus requires a higher return, than a share in the same company that enables the owner to influence who sits on the board and to hold management accountable for its performance."[16] For two companies that are similar except for the rights of shareholders, the cost of equity will be higher for the company with few ownership rights than it will be for the company with strong rights. For example, empirical studies have generally shown that stock prices fall (that is, the cost of equity rises) when states enact antitakeover laws or when managers adopt antitakeover measures such as poison pills.[17] These measures usually restrict the power of shareholders to replace existing directors. Because the voting power of shareholders is stronger in Japanese and German companies than in U.S. companies, it would be natural to expect that the cost of equity would be higher for U.S. companies.

In fact, in the United States different states attract different kinds of companies. Delaware attracts large established companies; California attracts the largest number of incorporations and by far the largest number of new firms going public because it has never had an antitakeover statute.[18] This pattern of incorporation suggests that the corporate governance structure with strong shareholders' power in California reduces the cost of capital for growing companies.

16. Jacobs (1991, p. 195).
17. Easterbrook and Fischel (1991, p. 221).
18. Easterbrook and Fischel (1991, p. 223).

Figure 3-1. *Real After-Tax Cost of Debt, Four Advanced Industrial Countries, 1977–92*

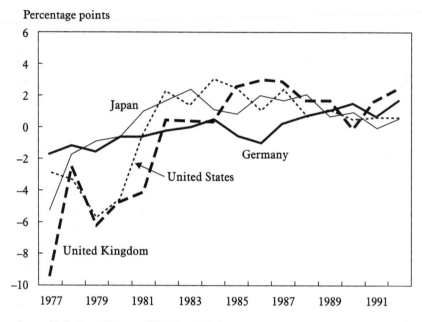

Source: McCauley and Zimmer (1994, chart 7-1).

Japan and Germany seem to have enjoyed considerably lower cost of capital than did the United States and the United Kingdom in the 1980s.[19] This was the result of higher leverage, a much lower cost of equity in Japan, and a lower cost of German companies' debt to banks. Closer bank-customer relationships and more stable prices and growth rates in Japan and Germany also seem to have lowered the cost of capital. Studies that cover the period since 1990 have found some tendency toward convergence in the cost of equity and capital.

Robert McCauly and Steven Zimmer have shown that the real costs of debt in the United States, Japan, and Germany converged during the 1980s (figure 3-1); this probably reflected the increas-

19. This discussion relies on Fukao (1993), which reviewed McCauley and Zimmer (1989, 1994), Ando and Auerbach (1991), Malkiel (1992), and Mattione (1992).

ing globalization of financial markets. Richard Mattione's study of the United States and Japan is consistent with this result, except that he suggests some widening in the differential during the 1990s.[20] The real costs of debt for companies with strong credit ratings are, then, converging. However, the corporate governance structure would affect the credit rating of a company with the same leverage incorporated in different countries, thus affecting the cost of capital.

Measuring the cost of equity empirically is more difficult than measuring the cost of debt. McCauley and Zimmer estimated the cost of equity for the United States, Japan, Germany, and the United Kingdom based on price-earnings ratios adjusted for such cross-country institutional differences as accounting standards, the level of cross-shareholding among firms, the growth rate, and the distortion of profits from inflation (figure 3-2).[21] Their estimates suggest that the cost was relatively low in Japan during the 1980s but that there has been a significant convergence during the 1990s. Burton Malkiel obtained slightly different results for the United States, Japan, and Germany based on share prices and future dividend payments as projected by security analysts (figure 3-2). His estimates show somewhat less difference between the United States, on the one hand, and Japan and Germany, on the other, and indicate that convergence began during the second half of the 1980s.

Measurements of leverage are usually based on the market value of equity and the book value of debt. The debt-equity ratios of U.S. and British firms have fluctuated around 1.0 for many years; those of Japanese and German firms have generally been much higher and are currently above 2.0 (figure 3-3). Most estimates show that the cost of equity is usually much higher than the cost of debt because interest payments are fully deductible for corporate tax purposes, whereas earnings are subject to corporate tax. Thus Japanese and German companies, which seem to be able to sustain greater leverage than U.S. or British firms, have an advantage with regard to their cost of capital.[22]

---

20. Mattione (1992).

21. McCauley and Zimmer (1989, 1994).

22. This advantage is at the level of individual companies and not an advantage at the national level. The lost tax revenue from a higher level of leverage in Japan and Germany has to be offset by higher taxes in other sectors of the economy.

Figure 3-2. *Estimated Real Cost of Equity, Four Advanced Industrial Countries, 1977–92*

McCauley and Zimmer estimate

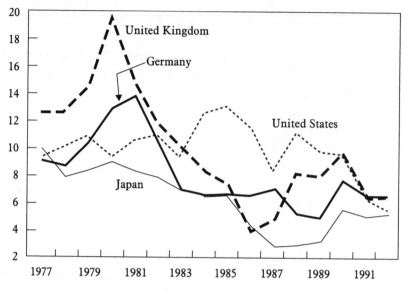

Malkiel estimate

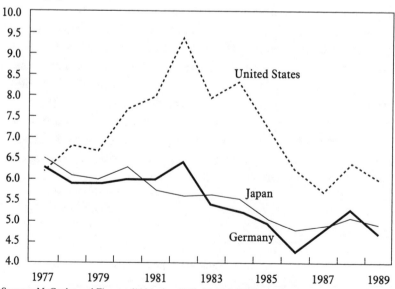

Sources: McCauley and Zimmer (1994, chart 7-2); Malkiel (1992, p. 12).

Figure 3-3. *Debt–Market Equity Ratios, Four Advanced Industrial Countries, 1977–92*

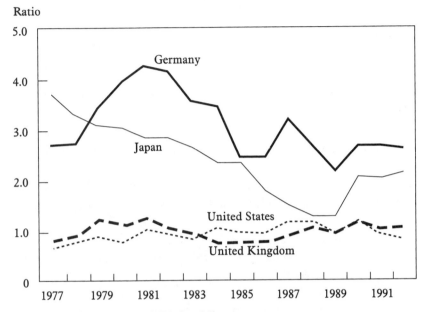

Source: McCauley and Zimmer (1994, chart 7-3).

The cost of funds reflects the combined impact of all the influences described so far. The cost of capital also takes account of the effects of the corporate tax system. Investment incentives such as tax credits and accelerated depreciation effectively lower the cost of investment projects and therefore reduce the cost of capital. Variations in corporate taxation among countries appear to have played a dwindling part in explaining international differences in the cost of capital.[23] This is due to the convergence of inflation rates at lower levels, which reduces a major source of distortion introduced by tax systems, and to tax reforms in a number of countries, including the United States,

23. See Commission of the European Communities (1992); and Fukao and Hanazaki (1987).

Germany, the United Kingdom, and Canada.[24] The general intent of these tax reforms has been to set depreciation allowances for tax purposes more realistically, to reduce or eliminate tax credits for investment, and to lower the tax rate.

McCauley and Zimmer have reported that businesses in Japan and Germany appear to have enjoyed considerably lower cost of funds than have businesses in the United States and the United Kingdom in the 1980s. For Japanese firms, this advantage was created by greater leverage and, during the second half of the decade, a much lower cost of equity, reflecting high stock prices in the Tokyo market. For German firms, the advantage was due to greater leverage and the lower cost of interest on short-term debt to banks. McCauley and Zimmer have also reported a tendency toward convergence in the cost of funds since the beginning of 1990 (figure 3-4).[25] As far as Japan is concerned, this largely reflects the sharp fall of stock prices on the Tokyo exchange.

Because the cost of capital takes account of tax incentives, it varies according to the type of investment project and the tax treatment to which it is subject. Figure 3-5 shows the sum of the cost of economic depreciation and the cost of capital (the "user" cost of capital). The trends in the cost of capital are broadly similar to those in the cost of funds.

Because the cost of funds in Japan and Germany is lower than in the United States and the United Kingdom, Japanese and German companies have been better able to invest in projects with a longer period of cost recovery. For instance, 47 percent of U.S. companies would not start a new business unless, from the beginning, it were more profitable than the current average return, but 56 percent of Japanese companies would start one if its return were higher than the current average return over the medium to long term (table 3-6). In other words, Japanese

24. A higher inflation rate tends to increase the size of tax distortions on debt finance. For a given real interest rate, when the rate of inflation increases, the nominal interest rate increases by the same amount. Although the increased interest payments can be deducted from taxable income, the effective capital gain from the reduction in the real value of outstanding borrowings is not taxable, reducing a company's total tax liability.

25. McCauley and Zimmer (1989, 1994).

Figure 3-4. *Real After-Tax Cost of Funds, Four Advanced Industrial Countries, 1977–92*

Percentage points

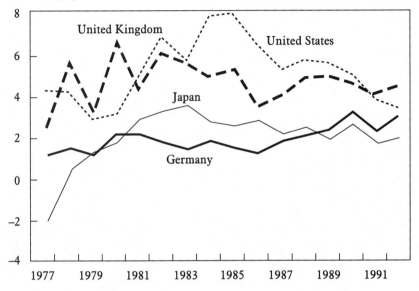

Source: McCauley and Zimmer (1994, chart 7-4).

companies discount future returns on investment less than U.S. companies do.

Human Resource Policy

Made in America, an influential MIT study on the performance of U.S. manufacturing industries, identified neglect of human resources as the major cause of the weakness of the U.S. manufacturing sector compared with those of Japan and Germany. In U.S. companies employing traditional mass production techniques, tasks are divided into small elements that can be performed by unskilled workers who are treated as replaceable parts. Training is usually brief and focused on specific, narrow skills that are immediately put into service. Workers are often treated as a cost to be controlled, not as an asset to be developed.[26]

26. Dertouzos and others (1989, p. 86).

Figure 3-5. *User Cost of Capital for Two Types of Investment,*
Four Advanced Industrial Countries, 1977–91

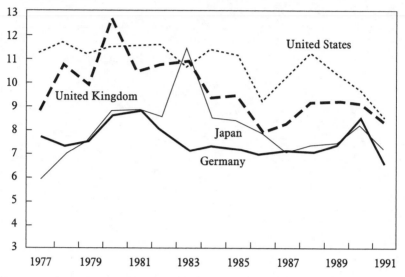

Equipment and machinery with physical life of 20 years

Percentage points

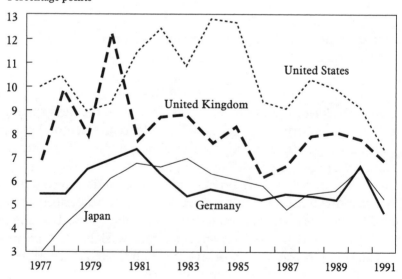

Factory with physical life of 40 years

Percentage points

Source: McCauley and Zimmer (1994, table 7-2).

Table 3-6. *Attitudes toward Profitability and Starting a New Line of Business, U.S. and Japanese Companies, 1988*

Attitude	U.S. companies	Japanese companies
Would start a new line of business if it were not loss-making over medium to long term	29.4	34.5
Would start a new line of business if its return were higher than the current average return over the medium to long term	23.5	55.5
Would not start a new line of business unless it were more profitable than the current average return from the beginning	47.1	10.0

Source: Kigyo Kodo ni Kansuru Chosa Kenkyu Iinkai (1988, p. 16). The table is based on a questionnaire sent to large manufacturing companies in Japan and the United States.

On-the-job training is emphasized much more in Japanese and German companies. In Germany most sixteen-year-olds enter apprenticeships on leaving school. The apprentice spends an average of three years working under a trained instructor and is given additional schooling. National examinations certify the successful completion of an apprenticeship. Further promotions require specific job experience, further schooling, and the certification of an additional examination. In Japan, education and training for specific jobs and for promotion are planned and provided by individual firms. General skills, which are often firm specific, are acquired primarily by rotation through various departments. Most large companies maintain training centers, and most employees spend several days there each year. Participation in worker circles to improve quality also helps improve employee capabilities. Broad skills improve productivity both directly and indirectly. Skilled workers generally exploit new systems more fully and reliably. They can function with less oversight and can manage unusual circumstances such as the malfunction of machines without outside help.[27]

27. Dertouzos and others (1989, pp. 87–90).

In traditional mass production, of automobiles for example, a great many interchangeable parts are assembled by unskilled workers to produce a single product. Quality is maintained by inspection and correction efforts at the end of the production line, a process that is costly. Assembly workers are not expected to fix problems on the production line—specialists are employed for the purpose. In so-called lean production systems, however, parts are assembled by teams of workers who know the production process well.[28] They are expected to rectify problems on the production line immediately and to suggest improvements in the production process. The maintenance of quality is thus built into the production system, and corrections at the end of the line are rarely needed. And, because of the greater skills of production workers, different models can be assembled on a single line.

An extensive comparative study of auto assembly plants in Japan, North America, and Europe has shown an enormous difference in human resource management policy and productivity (table 3-7). Japanese companies provide 370 to 380 hours of training to new production workers; American companies provide 46 hours. Job rotation is much more frequent in Japanese plants than in American plants. This investment in workers, in combination with the lean production system, supports higher productivity and better quality in Japanese plants. Although the Japanese-owned plants in North America perform relatively well in terms of productivity and quality, the number of suggestions from employees lags far behind those in plants in Japan. The performance of European plants is less impressive both in productivity and in quality, although they provide almost four times more hours of training than U.S. plants provide. This difference of performance between Japanese and European manufacturers is due to the European auto manufacturers' lack of familiarity with the lean production system.

The lean production system is supported by managements' commitments to long-term employment:

---

28. The contrast of lean production and traditional mass production is extensively explained in Womack, Jones, and Roos (1990).

Table 3-7. *Assembly Plant Characteristics of Volume Auto Producers, by Region, 1989*[a]

Characteristic	Japanese plants in Japan	Japanese plants in North America	American plants in North America	All Europe
Performance				
Productivity (hours per vehicle)	16.8	21.2	25.1	36.2
Quality (assembly defects per 100 vehicles)	60.0	65.0	82.3	97.0
Layout				
Space (sq. ft. per vehicle per year)	5.7	9.1	7.8	7.8
Inventories (days for eight sample parts)	0.2	1.6	2.9	2.0
Work force				
Job rotation (0 = none, 4 = frequent)	3.0	2.7	0.9	1.9
Suggestions per employee	61.6	2.7	0.9	1.9
Training of new production worker (hours)	380.3	370.0	46.4	173.3

Source: Womack, Jones, and Roos (1990, p. 92).

a. Averages for plants in each region.

in the end, it is the dynamic work team that emerges as the heart of the lean factory. Building these efficient teams is not simple. First, workers need to be taught a wide variety of skills—in fact, all the jobs in their work group so that tasks can be rotated and workers can fill in for each other. Workers then need to acquire many additional skills: simple machine repair, quality-checking, housekeeping, and materials-ordering. Our studies of plants trying to adopt lean production reveal that workers respond only when there exists some sense of reciprocal obligation, a sense that management actually values skilled workers, will make sacrifices to retain them, and is willing to delegate responsibility to the team.[29]

Thus the relatively senior position of the claims of Japanese workers to the company's assets is an indispensable factor in maintaining an efficient lean production system. This senior position of

29. Womack, Jones, and Roos (1990, p. 99).

workers is maintained by the mostly implicit contract between core employees and management. The workers' commitment is reinforced by the difficulty of finding other jobs for those in mid-career.

The Japanese employment system has its own costs. First, it is very expensive for employers to maintain a large number of core workers during prolonged recessions. Although recessions in Japan have been relatively short and mild with a high underlying growth rate, this experience is likely to change. Second, except for highly skilled professionals such as foreign exchange dealers or software engineers, it is difficult and disadvantageous to change jobs in mid-career. Consequently, businesses cannot expand rapidly by hiring experienced workers. Third, it is very difficult to have a market for corporate control without changing the fundamental structures of Japanese companies. If, because of the threat of corporate takeovers, management could not provide a credible long-term commitment to workers, it would be very hard to convince workers to spend time and effort to acquire firm-specific skills.

The U.S. system does have some advantages in comparison with the Japanese system. Although the seniority system is not flexible enough to adopt lean production techniques, it can facilitate rapid shrinkage of employment during recessions because it allows employers to release less experienced workers and retain a core of more experienced ones. Workers also have a strong incentive to acquire skills that are in demand in the market. At the same time, however, companies find it difficult to maintain the loyalty of employees and to convince them to acquire firm-specific skills. Employees' lack of commitment through the acquisition of firm-specific skills in turn relegates their claim on a company's assets to a very subordinate position. Workers are consequently treated as a variable cost of production and are laid off as soon as production falls. An active job market reinforces the fluidity of the situation.

Although the U.S. job market seems a harsh environment for employees, it is not necessarily so for all workers. For talented professionals and skilled workers, it is full of opportunities. In a fluid market, even mid-career workers can obtain high-paying jobs.

They may face unexpected termination of employment, but they can find new opportunities in growing sectors of the economy. Talented workers may very well be better off working with a dynamic growing company at some risk of temporary unemployment than having strong job security with a declining company.

Long-Term Relationships among Companies

As with labor-management relationships, there are large differences in the relationships among companies in America and Japan.[30] American automobile manufacturers, for example, use two ways to obtain parts: they maintain vertically integrated in-house supply divisions and let out short-term contracts with suppliers who are kept at arm's length. American assemblers are much more vertically integrated than Japanese assemblers. With 850,000 employees worldwide, General Motors added 70 percent of the value of 8 million vehicles. With 37,000 employees, Toyota added only 27 percent of the value of 4 million vehicles.[31] U.S. manufacturers have traditionally sent out parts specifications to many suppliers for bids. The contracts offered are for relatively short periods, and assemblers have often shifted orders to lower-cost suppliers at short notice. Suppliers often have little incentive to invest in assembler-specific capital goods for product innovations.[32]

In Japan, auto manufacturers select a relatively small number of suppliers and maintain close relationships with them. First-tier suppliers are typically asked to design and deliver whole vehicle systems. To ensure a high level of effort, assemblers often divide their parts order between several suppliers—so-called face-to-face competition. When a supplier's product fails to meet quality or reliability standards, an assembler may shift some business to other sources as a penalty. But assemblers usually retain their suppliers

30. The following example of automobile industries is taken from Asanuma (1992), Womack, Jones, and Roos (1990), and Dertouzos and others (1989).

31. See Womack, Jones, and Roos (1990, p. 155).

32. In recent years, after observing the merit of Japanese-style relationships between assemblers and suppliers, U.S. auto manufacturers have started to use more long-term contracts with a smaller number of suppliers. See Womack, Jones, and Roos (1990, p. 161).

as long as they make efforts to improve. Thus suppliers are often regarded as fixed costs, like the assemblers' employees.

The Japanese system requires very close communication between assemblers and suppliers and strong commitments on both sides. This long-term relationship is supported by ownership of stock in one another's companies, exchanges of personnel, customer-specific investment by suppliers, assemblers' reliance on a few suppliers for indispensable components, and technical assistance provided by assemblers to suppliers.[33] Typically, assemblers, as a part of normal job rotation, send middle managers to their suppliers to facilitate communication. Stable employment in Japan makes it easier to make flexible long-term implicit contracts among companies, an advantage in modern manufacturing, where mass-marketed durable goods are almost invariably produced by networks of firms.[34]

The Welfare of Workers

Japanese companies have an advantage in investing in the broad training of workers and in keeping long-term commitments among networks of companies, but the system has disadvantages. For one thing, management's commitment to provide stable employment and the effort by employees to honor this commitment with hard work have blurred the distinction between private and business life. The personal network of trust within a company and with managers of related companies has become many managers' most important asset. To maintain it, they spend endless hours socializing with colleagues in their own company and related companies. This manifests itself in long meetings, drinking after work, weekend golf with customers, and so on. The emphasis on teamwork in performance evaluation also encourages employees to avoid placing an extra burden on fellow workers by taking leave; a large part of paid leave in Japan remains unused.[35]

33. Miwa (1989); and Ito (1989).
34. Kester (1992).
35. Average use of paid leave is only nine days, in spite of entitlement to about twenty; Nihon Keizai Shinbun-sha (1990, p. 140).

Table 3-8. *Index of Production Worker and Office Worker Wages in Three Industrialized Countries, by Age*
Average wage = 100

	Production workers			Office workers		
Age	Japan[a]	United Kingdom[b]	Germany[c]	Japan[a]	United Kingdom[b]	Germany[c]
20–24	73.5	86.5	97.2	59.6	64.6	70.4
25–29	87.0	98.3	102.6	74.5	86.0	91.5
30–34	98.8	106.8	105.0	89.8	106.3	104.5
35–39	111.4	106.8	105.2	103.5	106.3	109.3
40–44	119.9	108.6	103.9	116.4	118.5	110.2
45–49	125.7	108.6	102.5	129.0	118.5	106.5
50–54	124.3	101.2	100.1	134.9	109.2	104.9
55–59	109.9	101.2	97.0	124.6	109.2	101.3
60–64	81.3	90.9	93.2	91.7	90.7	100.6
65 or older	68.1	90.9	93.2	76.0	90.7	100.6

Source: Based on data in Keizai Kikaku Cho (1992, pp. 268, 504).
a. Male workers in manufacturing in 1991.
b. Male full-time workers in all industries in 1991.
c. Male workers in manufacturing in 1992.

The structure of wages and salaries in Japanese companies, designed to further enforce a long-term commitment on the part of employees, can also be a burden on employees.[36] Wages increase more steeply for workers aged twenty to fifty-four than they do at companies in the United Kingdom and Germany (table 3-8). This wage structure can be partly explained by employees' accumulation of skill, but that does not explain it fully. The result is sometimes also interpreted as under-compensation for young workers to encourage them to stay with one company, and it works. But the undercompensation is also in effect an invisible investment by young workers in the company, an investment without portability and secured only by an implicit contract with management. Undercompensation is counteracted by overcompensation for senior workers accord-

36. The following discussion depends on the excellent analysis of Kagono and Kobayashi (1989).

ing to their long-term performance and a severance payment whose size is linked to length of tenure in the company.[37]

The Japanese structure of wages and salaries thus effectively aligns incentives for employees with the long-term stable growth of the company to protect their investment. But it limits personal freedom. When employees are unlikely to resign from a company, management can exercise stronger control over them. Consequently, most Japanese permanent employees accept overtime hours, job rotations, and transfers to faraway positions, often without their families. This system is sustainable only when workers value job security and the prospects of promotion more than their freedom and their private lives. (For these reasons the system has become one of the major deterrents that keep women from having professional careers in Japanese companies.)

Reflecting these characteristics, the average duration of employment with one company is longer in Japan than it is in other major countries. Studies in the 1970s and 1980s estimated that the average duration of employment was 7.2 years in the United States, 8.5 in the United Kingdom, 9.5 in France, 10.0 in Germany, and 12.3 in Japan.[38] For all age groups, the duration is much longer in Japan than in the United States (table 3-9). The ratio of employees in Japanese manufacturing companies who have never changed their job is extremely high; 49 percent for high-school graduates 45–49 years old and 55 percent for university graduates of the same age (table 3-10). The average number of hours worked by an employee at a Japanese company is the highest among the five major countries because of the great amounts of overtime worked and the paid leave that goes unused (table 3-11).

Thus Japanese management does its best to avoid laying off permanent employees by giving the claims of core workers precedence over those of shareholders. At the same time, employees have to accept long working hours, varied job assignments, and a

---

37. According to a model contract created by the Kansai Region Corporate Management Conference in 1982, an office worker with a university diploma should receive a severance payment of 5.1 months of salary for 10 years of tenure, 15.9 months for 20 years, 31.6 months for 30 years, and 37.9 months for 32 years (retirement). See Aoki (1992, p. 67).

38. Keizai Kikaku Cho (1992, p. 265).

Table 3-9. *Duration of Employment with One Company in Japan and the United States, by Age and Sex, 1980s*

Percent

Sex and age		0–1	2–4	5–9	10–14	15–19	20 or more
				Years of employment			
				United States			
Male	15–24	56.1	39.6	3.9	0.4	0	0
	25–34	27.6	43.0	17.9	10.4	1.0	0.1
	35–44	16.8	26.3	14.8	20.0	15.4	6.9
	45–54	11.1	17.3	10.9	14.3	13.5	32.8
	55–64	8.9	14.5	8.4	12.3	11.2	44.7
Female	15–24	56.7	40.9	2.3	0.2	0	0
	25–34	33.1	43.2	15.4	7.6	0.7	0
	35–44	24.3	37.7	15.6	12.7	7.1	2.7
	45–54	15.5	30.3	16.1	17.3	10.6	10.3
	55–64	10.8	22.8	14.4	18.6	12.8	20.7
				Japan			
Male	15–24	12.5	67.0	20.5	0	0	0
	25–34	2.7	24.5	40.8	25.2	6.7	0
	35–44	1.3	8.8	11.8	20.2	29.6	28.2
	45–54	1.2	6.8	7.8	9.2	11.0	64.1
	55–64	3.0	16.2	11.9	8.0	7.4	53.4
Female	15–24	12.3	71.5	16.2	0	0	0
	25–34	6.3	32.5	40.1	18.4	2.7	0
	35–44	6.5	31.4	24.9	15.7	13.5	8.1
	45–54	3.3	20.4	24.3	20.9	11.8	19.3
	55–64	2.4	15.9	18.1	18.3	13.5	31.9

Source: Keizai Kikaku Cho (1992, p. 503).

deep commitment to the long-term stable growth of the company. This system may be fragile during a severe cyclical downturn of the economy. If many large Japanese companies were forced to lay off large numbers of core employees, the credibility of the implicit employment contract would be permanently impaired. But the basic structure of the system has been maintained by built-in flexibility, and it has withstood the severe business downturn that began in 1991.

If the dark side of the labor management policy of Japanese companies has been relatively unknown, the dark side of American

Table 3-10. *Male Employees in Japan Who Have Never Changed Jobs,
by Age, Sector, and Educational Attainment, 1980–85*
Percent

Age	High school graduates		University graduates	
	Manufacturing	Service	Manufacturing	Service
19 or younger	100.0	100.0	...	...
20–24	73.1	53.0	100.0	100.0
25–29	65.6	37.6	84.9	76.4
30–34	61.0	33.6	73.5	59.7
35–39	57.4	29.3	67.6	48.3
40–44	53.8	22.7	63.5	41.3
45–49	49.3	21.5	55.4	35.7
50–54	45.6	16.2	40.7	26.2
55–59	25.7	9.4	19.5	14.4
60–64	4.6	1.9	3.5	6.3
65 or older	1.5	0.4	0.9	1.2

Source: Aoki (1992, p. 76).

labor management policy has been all too familiar. Employment is
generally less stable and frictional unemployment higher in the
United States than in Japan. High adjustment costs of moving to a
new job are primarily borne by unemployed workers. Companies
and workers invest less in company-specific skills in the United
States. In a sense these are the costs management and labor must
pay for avoiding a strong commitment to stable employment in
favor of greater flexibility and adaptability.

Table 3-11. *Average Hours Worked per Year by Workers in Five Industrial
Countries, 1980, 1985, 1990*

Country	1980	1985	1990
United States	1,893	1,929	1,948
Japan	2,162	2,168	2,124
Germany	1,719	1,663	1,598
France	1,759	1,644	1,683
United Kingdom	1,883	1,910	1,953

Source: Keizai Kikaku Cho (1992, p. 506).

Efficient Redeployment of Capital and Workers

Given the differences in the organization of companies in Japan (and probably Germany) and the United States, one also expects differences in the efficiency of redeploying capital and labor from economic activities that are no longer profitable. Japan (and probably Germany) shows relatively smooth movements of labor and capital within a company but more sluggish movements among them. The United States (and probably the United Kingdom) shows relatively smooth movements of labor and capital among companies.

Because Japanese workers accommodate the requests of management to maintain stable employment, labor can be efficiently reallocated within a company. However, the expansion or contraction of the total employment of a company is slower than it is in the United States. And because legal restrictions on the distribution of paid-in capital to shareholders are also strict in Japan, the free cash flow of mature industry is not easily paid out as dividends.[39] When a mature company's profitability declines, the free cash flow is often used to protect core employees at the expense of shareholders. For example, Nippon Steel's management worked hard to "satisfy expectations of lifetime employment of skilled workers in the face of receding growth and threatened profitability of the company's core business. Unrelated diversification plans in progress [in 1991] are arguably more to the advantage of Nippon Steel's current employees than to the suppliers of capital and could, therefore, set the stage of further stakeholder conflicts."[40]

In other words, Japanese companies tend to internalize both frictional or temporary unemployment and cyclical unemployment by trying to redeploy excess workers, sometimes at the expense of shareholders. On the positive side, these adjustment efforts create strong internal pressures for expansion and diversification of the company. They also reduce the burden of unemploy-

---

39. Free cash flow is cash flow in excess of that required to fund all of a firm's projects that have a positive net present value when discounted at the relevant cost of capital. See Jensen (1988).

40. Kester (1991, p. 170).

ment for the government and individual households. But on the negative side, the efforts may result in the inefficient use of capital and may limit the potentially more efficient use of labor by inhibiting intercompany movements of workers. The thin labor market for mid-career workers also makes it difficult to start a new company.

American companies tend to externalize the adjustment costs by relying on outright layoffs. Free cash flow can be returned to shareholders either by large dividends or by stock repurchases. Shareholders can then reinvest this money in new businesses. And the abundant supply of mid-career workers in the labor market makes it easy to start these new businesses. Still, the existence of high rates of frictional unemployment in the United States relative to rates in Japan creates political pressure to avoid unemployment and accommodate some inflation.

Reflecting these differences in corporate behavior, large companies in Japan often begin new lines of business as a diversification strategy, but in the United States young venture companies are the ones that begin new businesses. The spectacular growth of young companies such as Apple, Microsoft, and Intel is common in the United States; it is far less common in Japan.

Newcomers, either foreign or domestic, find it far more difficult to establish themselves in Japanese markets than in American markets. The tendency of Japanese companies to value long-term relationships between manufacturers and suppliers instead of spot transactions tends to freeze out new market entrants, including foreign companies. Once established, however, a company can enjoy more stable business and greater profits in Japan. According to one observer, Japanese subsidiaries of such U.S. companies as Levi Strauss, Kentucky Fried Chicken, and Avon realized higher price-earnings multiples when their stocks were offered in Japanese markets than their parent companies realized in U.S. markets.[41]

But it is easier for a new company to start a business and to expand in U.S. markets. Companies less than ten years old made up just 0.7 percent of all companies that floated shares in the over-the-counter (OTC) market in Japan in the 1980s, compared

41. Fikre (1991).

with 40 percent in the United States.[42] The average Japanese company that floated shares in the Japanese OTC market was about twenty-nine years old; the average U.S. company in the NASDAQ was five years old.[43] The prevalence of short-term arm's length contracts with suppliers also makes it easier for new companies to grow in the U.S. market, growth aided by the relative ease with which they can hire workers with diverse experience. However, the profits of start-up companies in the United States are less stable, and they often have difficulty committing labor and capital to long-term projects. As a result, after showing a strong initial growth, a new U.S. company often fails to become a stable and strong concern.[44]

42. Nihon Keizai Shinbun-sha (1990, p. 483).

43. "Tento shijo, hirogaru nichi-bei kakusa," *Yomiuri Shinbun,* May 7, 1994.

44. The "flash-in-the-pan pattern" in the American semiconductor industry was emphasized in Dertouzos and others (1989, pp. 9–10).

Chapter 4

Conclusions and Policy Recommendations

PRESSURES for change in the structures of corporate governance come from two sources: the globalization of production processes and the integration of world financial markets. Globalization of production is encouraging corporations from various countries to adopt the most efficient elements of each others' systems. The integration of financial markets has encouraged greater harmonization in disclosure and stock market rules.

Globalization of Production

In modern manufacturing, mass-marketed durable goods are produced by networks of production plants. In the United States, companies have traditionally used variants of two primary forms to organize these networks: vertical integration of production processes and short-term, arm's-length transactions with suppliers and distributors. Japanese companies have avoided vertical integration and employed keiretsu-type, long-term arrangements. Although the merits of the keiretsu model have been appreciated by many observers, new businesses find that the long-term relationships make the Japanese market more difficult to penetrate. Probably the most desirable direction for Japanese and U.S. companies to develop is mutual recognition of different contractual forms and higher transparency in keiretsu transactions. In Japan it is necessary to balance the efficiency of long-term transactions with the flexibility generated by market contestability from newcomers.

A so-called exchange of hostages is often used as a framework for long-term transactions among Japanese companies: suppliers invest in plant and equipment to better serve a specific assembler, while the assembler relies on only a few suppliers for his indispensable components. A breach of trust would be too costly for either to gamble. If a supplier loses his customer, his expensive plant and equipment will lose most of their value. If an assembler abandons a supplier, production will be badly disrupted and his disloyalty will shake the confidence of his other suppliers.[1]

The exchange of hostages is very effective in reinforcing incentives for group cooperation. For this reason, reductions in the number of suppliers and greater reliance on long-term contracts have increasingly been adopted by U.S. and European companies.[2] But the approach has potential flaws. It can, for example, be used to restrict competition. Given the international competitiveness of Japanese manufacturing, the inefficiency due to restricted competition is probably not important in Japan's manufacturing sector. If, for example, keiretsu-type transactions were used to preserve inefficient companies in a production keiretsu, those companies would not be able to compete in the world market. However, a less exclusive approach in organizing a production keiretsu could be more efficient. More innovations in products and production could be expected if suppliers were less inbred.

The possibility of abuse of the keiretsu relationship is likely to be greater in situations in which the locus of power is one-sided: strong assemblers versus a diversity of dealers, concentrated wholesalers versus dispersed retailers. Long-term transactions in the distribution system tend to result in noncompetitive practices such as the wholesalers' exclusion of competitors' products and arrangements for maintaining retail prices at artificially high levels. If collusive boycotting of goods from foreign companies or limita-

---

1. On the exchange of hostages, see Ito (1989) and Williamson (1985, chap. 8).

2. American auto manufacturers have reduced the number of suppliers from 2,000–2,500 at the beginning of the 1980s to 1,000–1,500 at the end (Womack, Jones, and Roos (1990, p. 157). The Volkswagen group plans to reduce the number of suppliers from the current 2,300 to 100–200 by the year 2000 (Kevin Done, "Sharp Reduction in Number of Component Suppliers Planned," *Financial Times,* June 10, 1993, p. 28).

tion of transactions to a favored few suppliers is used to create nontariff barriers, stronger antitrust measures must be applied.[3] Thus, as a result of the Structural Impediments Initiative (SII), the application of the antitrust law has been reinforced.[4] If keiretsu transactions are used appropriately and the arrangements are transparent, collusive boycotting or discrimination against outside competition can be avoided and efficiency enhanced.

For its part the United States, in the application of its antitrust policy, has to take account of the potential efficiency gains to be realized from keiretsu-type transactions.[5] In the past, U.S. regulatory agencies have permitted a very high level of vertical integration. Because of vertical integration in the automobile industry, for example, the growth of strong and viable parts suppliers was inhibited. Traditionally, all contractual forms that are not arm's-length and spot transactions have been suspected as anticompetitive contracts.[6] But recent theoretical developments have shown that many of these contracts improve efficiency. A more practical and less dogmatic application of antitrust policy is urgently required.

Global Integration of Financial Markets

The increasing integration of financial markets has also been exerting pressure for institutional changes on the part of the vari-

3. The Fair Trade Commission of Japan found anticompetitive keiretsu arrangements between the distributors of automobiles, automobile parts, sheet glass, and paper and their manufacturers. For example, keiretsu wholesalers threatened to cut off the supply of sheet glass to retailers who had started to sell imported glass. The commission intends to stop such practices by stronger enforcement of antitrust legislation (*Nihon Keizai Shinbun*, June 30, 1993).

4. The SII was launched by President Bush and Prime Minister Uno in July 1989 to identify and solve structural problems in both countries that stand as impediments to trade and balance of payment adjustments. The final report was issued in June 1990.

5. Dertouzos and others (1989, pp. 105–06) pointed out that the fear of antitrust action had inhibited cooperation among companies that was potentially beneficial for the U.S. economy. The authors appreciated the enactment of the National Cooperative Research Act in 1984 and recommended a further selective relaxation of antitrust restrictions.

6. Williamson (1985, p. 17) states that "until very recently the primary economic explanation for nonstandard or unfamiliar business practice was monopoly." Coase (1972, p. 67) also wrote that "if an economist finds something—a business practice of one sort or another—that he does not understand, he looks for a monopoly explanation."

ous forms of corporate governance. Equity portfolios are rapidly becoming internationally diversified. Issuers of equity, even those companies that have traditionally limited their shareholders to domestic investors, have encouraged internationalization of their investor bases as a means of improving their liquidity and reducing funding costs. Investors have sought more stable returns through portfolio diversification. In response to these trends most major countries have eliminated restrictions on foreign investment in securities of their domestic companies, and others are following.

These trends have put pressure on companies to disclose their accounts in a form that allows comparison across national boundaries. At present, disclosure rules, including accounting rules, vary greatly among corporations in various countries. But companies that have increasingly multinational investor bases, as well as those that would like to expand their bases in that direction, face pressure from creditors and shareholders to disclose their performance in a more uniform fashion.

Countries have also felt pressure to change laws to encourage and accommodate increased foreign investment. In 1992 Sweden rescinded a law that required non-Swedes to obtain permission from the public authorities to acquire voting shares beyond a certain limit.[7] In Switzerland many large companies are attracting foreign investors by improving disclosure practices and simplifying equity structure. Chemical giants Ciba-Geigy, Roche Holding, and Sandoz and food company Nestle have adopted the accounting guidelines issued by the London-based International Accounting Standards Committee.[8] In September 1993, when Daimler-Benz became the first German company to be fully listed on the New York Stock Exchange, the company reported accounts under the U.S. generally accepted accounting principles (GAAP) as well as under the German rules.[9] Japan's rigid accounting system,

7. Robert Taylor, "Sweden Loses Fear of Capital Inflow," *Financial Times,* February 13, 1993, p. 7.

8. Ian Rodger, "Stepping Out on to a Wider Stage," *Financial Times,* February 6, 1992, p. 21.

9. Peter Norman and John Gapper, "Germany Seeks U.S. Concession on Listings," *Financial Times,* September 27, 1993, p. 21.

which inhibits off-balance-sheet transactions and distorts reported profits, has forced many companies, including Japanese banks, to set up foreign subsidiaries to circumvent the rules. These movements toward more internationally comparable disclosure statements will aid in the more efficient allocation of capital. Policymakers can play a constructive role by assisting them.

There has also been pressure on financial authorities to adopt adequate insider trading rules to protect small shareholders and avoid manipulations of the market by corporate insiders. Shareholders have wanted to have rules to treat all shareholders equally. National authorities have competed to have an efficient and trusted national financial market so as to promote the securities business. Japan's tightening of insider trading rules in 1988 and Germany's introduction of them in 1994 reflect these movements. Some convergence in these rules and enforcement processes is likely to continue. But although it is desirable to have adequate rules against insider trading, it is necessary to recognize the need for close communication between management and large shareholders so that companies can be better governed. Authorities have to strike a balance between these two objectives.

The increasing international activities of financial institutions have also created pressure for harmonizing differences in financial market structures. Mutual penetration of financial institutions under different regulatory regimes has created a difficult problem for monetary authorities. Banks from Germany, Switzerland, France, and other countries with universal banking systems want freedoms similar to those in countries such as the United States and Japan that have maintained the separation of banking and security businesses.

The evolution of market pressures and competition among authorities may also produce perverse results of convergence. The competition among national authorities to attract companies may result in corporate governance systems that are biased in favor of the managements in place. With increasingly diversified foreign ownership, the political power of shareholders would be diluted. And a company with a large employment force in a country has strong political power, which may force the country to protect the management and employees at the expense of shareholders. Control of corporate law by individual states in the United States shows such problems: directors can effectively change a corporate charter without shareholders' approval by lobbying for a change in the state corporate law. To avoid this potential problem, control of corporate law should be in the hands of a higher legislative body. It is conceivable to place control of U.S. corporate law in the hands of Congress, for example, or at least to have a federal corporate law with a good balance of power between management and shareholders. The European Union may face similar problems in the future, and the introduction of a common corporate law will become increasingly necessary.[10] This problem may become more serious as international equity portfolios become more diversified.

Although market-induced pressure and competition among authorities to attract sound securities business have achieved convergence in some aspects of corporate governance, more harmonization is needed in stock market rules, accounting rules, and bankruptcy procedures. The ensuing discussion reviews policy actions to improve this process, but the conclusions are highly tentative. A much deeper analysis would be required in the actual harmonization process.

Current U.S. rules seem too restrictive of necessary information flows between large shareholders and management. Corporate governance in the United States would probably benefit from a clearer definition of insider trading because communications between shareholders and management would be safer and freer. Japan, Germany, and some European countries, which did not have adequate regulations against insider trading until recently, have tightened the rules in the past several years. Further modifications of these rules will be required, but it is not advisable for these countries to have excessively severe insider trading rules, given the rules' weakening effects on effective corporate governance.

---

10. One of the draft regulations of the European Union concerns a new type of company registered as an EU company that will be subject to EU laws. It will be called the Societas Europea (SE). In spite of pressure from the EU Commission, progress on this project is slow because member countries disagree about whether to allow worker participation on the boards of directors. See Nobes and Parker (1991, pp. 84–89).

Shareholders of companies targeted for takeovers need protection from abusive actions by both bidders and company management. Poison pills and other antitakeover measures deployed by U.S. companies have clearly strengthened the position of management at the cost of shareholders without changing the articles of incorporation. The United States would benefit by strengthening the stability and integrity of corporate structure, which are determined by the articles of incorporation and relevant corporate law. The United States could remove control of corporate law from the states and give it federal jurisdiction, or at least have a federal corporate law with a good balance of power between management and shareholders. Counties other than the United States and the United Kingdom will require more detailed takeover codes as their stock markets start to function as markets for corporate control.

International harmonization of disclosure requirements would facilitate more efficient allocation of capital. In this respect it is necessary to take account of the two objectives of an accounting system: to provide information to shareholders and creditors and to protect stakeholders of a company by maintaining enough capital to provide adequate security. Although it is useful to harmonize accounting rules to inform shareholders and creditors, it is not necessary to harmonize restrictions on the distribution of profits to shareholders. To achieve both the necessary harmony and the useful diversity, companies might estimate the amount of total shareholders' equity by using uniform international accounting rules to provide information and then to show two different parts of the equity—the distributable amount and the nondistributable amount—using accounting rules specific to each governance structure.

For a company with a large number of implicit contracts, it is very difficult to evaluate assets such as investment in human capital and some liabilities such as implicit employment contracts. This is an acute problem for Japanese and German companies, but a similar problem exists for U.S. companies. General Motors was recently required to make a large provision to cover future medical expenses of its retired workers. Although estimating these amounts as balances is difficult, net changes in total retirement benefits, net investment in training and research and development, and net contingency claims from suppliers should be included as much as possible as supplementary information in disclosure materials. If most implicit contracts can be disclosed by this procedure, a more realistic financial picture of Japanese and European companies could be achieved.

Increasingly frequent failures of multinational companies with complicated international creditor-debtor relationships will also necessitate more harmonized rules for bankruptcy procedures. For example, the risk of financial transactions is reduced by netting contracts, which are agreements to settle bilateral exposures with a single net payment in the event of a default of one of the parties. However, the enforceability of such contracts is not clear for cross-border transactions because of international differences in bankruptcy procedures. This problem is especially acute for financial institutions acting as intermediaries for many customers.[11] To reduce the systemic risks in international financial markets, it is also necessary to clarify the ambiguities in bankruptcy procedures. But the contractual priority among various classes of creditors in the harmonized bankruptcy procedure must be respected.

As mutual penetration of financial institutions proceeds, it is necessary to ensure that competition among financial institutions of various nationalities be fair. This is one of the objectives of the capital rule introduced in 1988 by the Bank for International Settlements. In the future, further harmonization of regulations on banks will be required.[12] For example, the current movement toward universal banks that combine security business and commercial banking is likely to continue, creating a potential conflict of interest. A universal bank could obtain repayment of loans from customers facing financial problems by getting them to issue securities. To avoid possible abuse by

11. This is one of the difficulties in implementing the Bank for International Settlements' capital rule for netting agreements on derivative transactions. The rule allows banks to keep a minimum capital calculated from their net credit exposures. However, this ambiguity in enforcing netting agreements makes it very difficult to estimate the net exposure. See Committee on Banking Regulations and Supervisory Practices (1988).

12. See Herring and Litan (1995).

banks, a stiff code of conduct with Chinese walls on the use of information would be necessary.

Current U.S. regulations on the separation of banking and commerce are excessive. Many observers advocate relaxing restrictions on shareholdings of nonfinancial companies by U.S. banks.[13] Although the control of banks by nonfinancial firms is very risky,[14] bank control of nonfinancial firms facing financial difficulties is occasionally observed in Germany and Japan and can be helpful in resolving companies' financial problems.

Fundamental Aspects of Corporate Governance

It is not desirable to have a piecemeal international harmonization of individual components of the structure of corporate governance because companies within each nation generally have a consistent structure. For example, it would be very difficult to have an open market for corporate control of established large companies in Japan or in Germany. A sudden change of management would likely result in a breach of implicit long-term contracts. One remedy might be to make these contracts more explicit and transparent to allow a more contestable market of corporate control in these countries. But the difficulties are too great.

Given the different comparative advantages of various corporate governance systems and their deep-rooted institutional backgrounds, it is neither desirable nor feasible to adopt a single system as a world standard. Each country should instead allow various complementary forms. French law, for example, allows two types of corporate structures: the traditional single-tier board and the German-style two-tier. At the time of incorporation, a company can choose the model that best suits its purpose. A venture company may want to choose the U.S. model, which allows very flexible restructuring in its paid-in capital. A manufacturing company may adopt the Japanese or Ger-

---

13. See Porter (1992, p. 82); Frankel and Montgomery (1991, p. 295); and Stiglitz (1985, p. 148).

14. The savings and loan crisis was exacerbated by real estate developers' effective control of federally insured banks.

man, which is conducive to more stable management. In every form of corporate governance, however, it is very important to strike a good balance of power among shareholders, the board of directors, and other stakeholders.

Corporate law may also allow a company to change its organizational model. As a company grows, it may want to adopt a different structure to respond to new needs and explore new activities. This reorganization must not, however, unduly disrupt the contractual relationships among its stakeholders. A change in the corporate model must also require the approval of its shareholders with a majority at least equal to that required for any other change in the articles of incorporation. When a change of structure may potentially weaken the payout restrictions of paid-in capital to shareholders, the company should obtain the approval of creditors as well.

Equitable Access in Corporate Takeovers?

The large wave of direct Japanese investment in U.S. companies in the late 1980s and the acquisition of U.S. companies by Japanese firms illuminated the absence of a market for corporate control in Japan. Often the one-sided flow of direct investment is cited as a manifestation of this problem. Table 4-1 shows the direct investment flows of advanced industrial countries. Japanese inward direct investment is by far the lowest among these countries in both 1971–80 and 1981–90. The boom in the acquisition of U.S. firms by the Japanese in the late 1980s was partially driven by the far cheaper cost of equity in Japan than in the United States. At the same time, many U.S. companies sold their equity stakes of Japanese companies to take advantage of very high stock prices in Japan: Chrysler sold Mitsubishi Automobile. Avon, Hughes Aircraft, Levi Strauss, Englehard, and PepsiCo floated shares of Japanese subsidiaries on the Tokyo market between 1987 and 1990. These transactions are recorded as negative foreign direct investment into Japan. The statistics of inward direct investment in Japan are also biased downward by the exclusion of retained earnings of foreign companies and the extensive use of tax haven countries by

Table 4-1. *Direct Investment Flows of Ten Major Countries, 1971–80, 1981–90*[a]

Cumulative flows as percent of nominal GDP at end of period

	1971–80	1981–90
United States		
Assets	4.96	3.20
Liabilities	2.08	6.43
Japan		
Assets	1.70	6.25
Liabilities	0.13	0.11
Germany		
Assets	3.07	5.65
Liabilities	1.72	1.10
France		
Assets	2.10	7.18
Liabilities	2.54	3.62
Italy		
Assets	0.79	2.57
Liabilities	1.26	2.31
United Kingdom		
Assets	10.27	19.17
Liabilities	7.63	12.43
Canada		
Assets	4.28	6.38
Liabilities	2.09	2.13
Belgium		
Assets	2.66	10.87
Liabilities	7.64	14.27
Netherlands		
Assets	11.38	18.38
Liabilities	5.12	9.86
Sweden		
Assets	3.68	20.18
Liabilities	0.72	3.64

Source: OECD statistics.

a. Retained earnings are not included for Japan, Germany, France, Italy, and Belgium.

foreign security companies established in Japan.[15] However, it is undeniable that the flow of net investment into Japan is low. Moreover, it is clearly easier for Japanese or German companies to take over U.S. or British firms than the contrary.

The core of the reason for the lack of a market for corporate control in Japan and probably in Germany is a large number of implicit contracts between the management of a company and its employees and subcontractors. In Japan these implicit contracts are protected by cross-shareholding. In Germany, representation of employees on supervisory boards, the control of proxy votes by large banks, and the small number of publicly traded companies makes unfriendly takeovers difficult.

One possible action to ease this situation is to have more explicit labor and other contracts. However, it would be very difficult to clarify all implicit contracts. And even if a foreign company could forcibly purchase a Japanese company, it would likely destroy the very fabric of closely knit corporate structure that generates the profits in the first place. To succeed, as Merck did when it purchased Banyu Pharmaceutical in 1983, a company must engage in a long period of confidence building so that existing implicit contracts can be inherited.[16]

Implications for Developing Countries and Former Centrally Planned Economies

Although the general structure of corporate governance remains similar in the five countries studied here, institutional details are often very important in determining the behavior of companies. The strong voting power of shareholders and good communication between them and management seem to have forged very

---

15. It is possible to estimate the retained earnings of U.S.-held Japanese companies from the difference between Japanese statistics, which do not include retained earnings, and U.S. statistics, which do. According to a study by the Japan Development Bank, statistics on U.S. direct investment to Japan are about three times larger than Japanese statistics of U.S. direct investment. This omission of retained earnings is much less important for the outward direct investment from Japan. See Sakurai (1991).

16. Kester (1991).

stable ownership of most Japanese and German companies. The ownership pattern of U.S. and British companies is less concentrated and less stable. As a result, the stock markets play the role of the market for corporate control in the United States and the United Kingdom but do not in Japan and Germany. Generally, management in Japanese and German companies is more stable and can offer more credible commitments to employees and suppliers than can management in U.S. and British companies. Finally, in Japan, Germany, and France paid-in capital is traditionally regarded more as security for creditors and other stakeholders of the company than as the property of shareholders.

These differences in the structure of corporate governance have a number of implications for the performance of companies. The strong voting power of shares appears to lower the cost of equity in Japan and Germany. Weaker voting power raises the cost in the United States and the United Kingdom. Strong restrictions on cash distributions to shareholders in Japan and Germany seem to lower the cost of debt and allow companies to maintain greater leverage. It seems easier for management in Japanese and German companies to maintain long-term implicit contracts with employees than it is for companies in the United States and the United Kingdom. Although the systems in Japan and Germany seem to allow firms in those countries to invest in more employee training, the pattern also makes deploying workers from declining sectors to growing ones more difficult.

I have not so far discussed the implications of this study for developing countries and former centrally planned economies, but an evaluation of advantages and disadvantages of different forms of corporate governance in the major industrial countries would be informative for policymakers building institutions in their economies. Public sale of shares in state-owned companies is not the end of privatization but only a beginning. Without a good governance mechanism, management in privatized companies can be as wasteful as that in any badly managed state-owned ones. Policymakers must therefore establish a workable governance structure for private companies. In this regard, corporate law, securities transaction law, and bankruptcy law have to be considered simultaneously because they have to be consistent with one another.

Given the relative merits and problems of the governance systems I have discussed, it would probably be easier for developing countries to implement the Japanese-German system. To have a workable U.S.- or British-style system, a country must have a well-functioning securities market and experienced accountants who can make sure that disclosure materials are accurate. Investors have to be familiar with the risks of investing in stock. The conditions necessary for a workable Japanese-German system are less stringent: a handful of large financial institutions that can assess credit risks.

Unfortunately, there is one important disadvantage for the Japanese-German system. The U.S. or British system can be learned from abundant English documents, but the Japanese-German system cannot. I hope that this study has demystified the latter system by explaining its strengths and weaknesses.

Comments

Colin Mayer

The past few years have witnessed a surge of interest in international comparisons of capital markets. Attention first focused on differences in the ways capital markets finance companies. More recently, studies have concentrated on the interrelation of corporate ownership, control, and governance. Mitsuhiro Fukao's study provides an excellent overview of this interrelation. It systematically records differences in the ways capital markets are organized and run. It discusses the structure of boards, ownership, markets for corporate control, accounting, and bankruptcy law. The appendix gives detailed information on individual countries that supplements the comparisons in the main text.

The author's thesis is that differences in the structure of capital markets affect the operation of corporate sectors. Shareholders are better placed to exercise corporate control in France, Germany, and Japan than they are in the United Kingdom and the United States. In Japan and Germany, especially, long-term shareholders wield significant power to nominate members of boards of directors and control executive compensation. In the United Kingdom and United States, shareholdings are dominated by pension funds. These institutional investors cannot easily communicate with each other because of insider trading rules, and they are restricted in their exercise of control because of antitrust regulations and takeover codes. As a consequence, corporate control is exercised through takeovers.

Colin Mayer is professor of management studies at the University of Oxford.

In France, Germany, and Japan, laws strictly limit companies' ability to make distributions out of paid-in capital, and conservative accounting conventions measure earnings and assets. Paid-in capital is regarded as security for stakeholders, including creditors. Creditors are afforded considerable protection under German and Japanese bankruptcy law but less protection under U.S. law.

Together these differences give rise to differences in the degree of protection stakeholders enjoy against downturns in corporate performance. In Japanese and continental European companies, bankruptcy laws protect creditors ahead of other stakeholders, and implicit contracts with stable owners protect a large number of core employees. In the United Kingdom and United States, executive compensation is protected by shareholders' weak control, and shareholders' dividends are protected ahead of the interests most employees and suppliers by accounting disclosure rules and weak regulation of distributions.

These differences affect the cost of capital, policy toward employees, and relations between companies. Long-term relations with banks and strong protection of creditors give rise to lower costs of capital in Japan and Germany. Long-term relations with employees mean that there is more investment in employee training in Germany and Japan and wider application of so-called lean systems of production. Long-term relations between companies encourage closer coordination between suppliers and purchasers.

Fukao notes that there are efficiency costs as well as benefits to the German-Japanese model. Employment decisions are inflexible, labor markets are thin, and corporate restructuring is difficult to achieve. There are also social costs in that employees must be more dedicated to long-term relations with their employers.

The author points to the pressures for change that come from the internationalization of markets. For example, he suggests that diversification of foreign ownership is weakening the power of shareholders relative to management. He advocates harmonization of insider trading rules, takeover rules, disclosure requirements, bankruptcy procedures, and the regulation of financial institutions. However, he does not believe that harmonization of corporate governance is appropriate, even if, in its absence, there are impediments to entry of foreign companies caused, for example, by takeover barriers. But it is unclear on which model of corporate governance it is desirable to harmonize, and attempts to eliminate barriers to entry of foreign firms confront fundamental differences in the structure and operation of corporate sectors.

What Fukao's discussion does is to point to a basic difference between Anglo-American capital markets, which mostly benefit shareholders and senior executives, and continental European and Japanese markets, which treat suppliers, purchasers, and employees as fixed instead of variable factors of production. The author attributes much of this disparity to regulation.

But on closer inspection it is not clear that the differences to which Fukao points are quite as pronounced or easy to classify as he suggests. For example, he himself notes that while the term of directors is comparatively long in France and Germany, it is short in Japan. And the roles of outside directors vary within as well as across countries. There are marked variations in the significance of nonexecutive directors in different U.K. companies. Again, while Germany has two-tier boards, Japan has one-tier boards; France has a mixture of the two.

Fukao argues that it is comparatively easy for shareholders to nominate members of the board in Germany and Japan. But he often suggests that the system of proxy votes in Germany confers effective control on banks. He states that shareholders have more influence on executive compensation in France, Germany, and Japan. However, some studies record that similar factors influence executive compensation in Germany, Japan, and the United States.[1]

As for ownership, although there are a small number of listed companies in France and Germany, there are a large number in Japan. Holdings by pension funds in the United Kingdom and United States are currently large, but this has not historically been the case. The relevance of insider trading rules to shareholder involvement is unclear. If shares are not traded, which is the feature of "participation" as against trade investments in Germany, then insider rules do not apply.

---

1. Kaplan (1993a, 1993b).

While it is frequently asserted that there are long-term share-holdings in Germany and Japan, there is evidence of significant sales of share stakes in France and Germany. Direct shareholdings by banks are small in Germany (approximately 8 percent in aggregate) and, although German banks can cast substantial proxy votes, these shares can be bought out by potential predators in takeovers.[2]

Fukao attaches considerable importance to differences in the size of the market for corporate control across countries. However, it is unclear that regulatory rules are the cause. For example, lax disclosure requirements allow predators in Germany to accumulate large toeholds (up to 25 percent) in targets without their being informed. There is also little protection of minority shareholders, so that targets can be purchased at comparatively low cost.

The author's pecking-order model relies on the protection afforded to creditors by bankruptcy laws. However, although Germany and Japan have creditor-oriented systems, France has a debtor-oriented system, and in the United Kingdom insolvency law protects creditors.

There are clearly significant differences in the structure of capital markets, and these differences affect corporate activities, but their source is difficult to pinpoint. Fukao does not really establish why implicit contracts, which are crucial to employee and corporate relations, can be sustained in Germany and Japan but not in the United Kingdom and United States. It is clear that takeovers cannot be the fundamental factor because, even in the United Kingdom and United States, the number of hostile as against accepted bids is small. As Masahiko Aoki has argued, different economic structures have to be treated as systems. Their historic origin is complex, and regulation is only one of several contributing factors.[3]

The direction of the pressures for changing capital markets may not be as clear as Fukao suggests. For example, the growth of international capital markets is normally thought to confer greater rather than diminished power on shareholders at the expense of

2. Franks and Mayer (1994).
3. Aoki (1994).

employees and managers by allowing investors to shift capital across national boundaries.

The author is correct to conclude that rules relating to corporate governance should not be harmonized across countries. In our current state of ignorance regarding the comparative merits of different financial systems, competition between systems rather than harmonization of them is appropriate. However, his proposal to harmonize other regulatory rules is of questionable value.

The normal economic justification for harmonization is that there are cross-border externalities: in the absence of harmonization, regulators in one country fail to take account of the effect of activities in their country on residents in other countries. If there are risks of the contagious spread of bank failures across countries, for instance, then bank regulation needs to be internationally harmonized. But this criterion of cross-border externalities does not apply to most of the areas to which the author refers. For example, provided that investors are aware of differences between markets, there is no reason why they should not be free to choose to invest in markets with few disclosure rules and little regulation of insider trading in just the same way as they are able to choose low-priced, low-quality products.

Finally, Fuako is too quick to extend his analysis of developed countries to eastern European countries. While in principle German- and Japanese-style market structures may be better suited to the needs of eastern European countries than are the stock market economies of the United Kingdom and United States, the problems of creating institutions like those of Germany and Japan are formidable. Eastern Germany has been able to construct its corporate sector on the back of western German institutions. For other eastern European countries the requirement that there be a "handful of large financial institutions that can assess credit risks" is proving to be a serious hurdle.

Michael E. Porter

Mitsuhiro Fukao's study provides a good description of the basic differences in the corporate governance structure in France, Germany, Japan, the United Kingdom, and the United States, with a special focus on the United States and Japan. The author recognizes, as I have, that the ownership and corporate governance structure in a country must be viewed as an internally consistent system.[1] The nature and size of ownership stakes, for example, affects the stability of shareholdings, which affects the nature of monitoring, which affects the types of information and disclosure demanded, and so on. What Fukao is less clear about is that the same consistency extends to internal management practices such as the hurdle rates used to evaluate investments, the manner in which the level and composition of executive and employee compensation is determined, the extent to which stable employment is maintained, how much is invested in training, and other practices.

Fukao's discussion of the individual elements of the capital allocation system (as I have termed it) of each country is accurate, but his treatment is incomplete in some important respects. For example, he sees the focus on quarterly reports in the United States as a manifestation of the difficulty of explaining intangible investments, but he underplays the crucial separation in the United States (and the United Kingdom) between the actual owner of equity and the institutional agent (a pension fund, for example, or a mutual fund) that makes investment decisions on the owner's behalf. The problem of selecting and monitoring agents contributes to the stunningly high rates of trading based on expectations of near-term price movements that characterize the U.S. market. The relative ease of takeover is another manifestation of these circumstances. Fukao is also silent on matters such as the duties of fiduciaries, the roles and influence of shareholders, and the role of boards of directors.

Michael E. Porter is a professor at Harvard Business School.

1. See Porter (1992).

Fukao states, and I agree, that no capital allocation system yet devised is unambiguously optimal. However, his discussion of the trade-offs involved in various countries' systems needs to be richer to make the implications of harmonization more clearly evident. For example, he portrays the Japanese system as supportive of lean production and other innovative management techniques and the U.S. system as not supportive. Yet this is clearly too simple. Many U.S. companies have adopted lean production and closer partnerships with suppliers in recent years. He also identifies the weaknesses of the Japanese system primarily in terms of its barriers to external competition and a tendency toward inefficient diversification to preserve employment. Yet Japanese diversification is primarily accomplished through internal development of new businesses rather than acquisitions, which results in a greater likelihood that businesses will enter into related businesses (with better results) than is the case in either the United States or the United Kingdom. Overall, therefore, Japanese diversification performance is better than U.S. performance. Conversely, Fukao fails to emphasize the high levels of inefficiency and overly broad product lines in many Japanese companies' core businesses.

Fukao implies that Japanese stockholders suffer in comparison with employees and other creditors. Yet Japanese stockholders have actually done well in a system that produces a higher rate of investment and hence growth than the U.S. system produces, while U.S. shareholders enjoy higher current profit rates but must accept slower growth and huge writeoffs due to downsizing. This confusion highlights a crucial issue that is missing from Fukao's discussion: the implications of different capital allocation systems for the rate of private sector investment in various forms, a particularly important matter for the long-term health of national economies. Harmonization that reduces the overall rate of investment would be truly unfortunate for the world economy.

In assessing the need for harmonization, Fukao takes a conservative approach with which I basically agree. Given the strong differences in the capital allocation systems in various countries and their deep institutional roots, it is both unlikely and undesirable to seek to harmonize them artificially. Moreover, the internal consistency among the various components of the system complicates harmonization because several changes must occur simultaneously and piecemeal changes can be counterproductive. The specific areas in which more harmonization is recommended— stock market rules, bankruptcy procedures, and some accounting rules—seem sensible. However, national practices in these areas are the way they are in part because of differences in the overall capital allocation system in the country. Insider trading rules will appropriately be less stringent in a system in which most shares are held by large, sophisticated, stable shareholders than they are in a system in which most shares are traded. The necessity for internal consistency also raises real questions about whether policies should converge toward the U.S. practice, the Japanese practice, or somewhere in between. In several places the author seems to argue implicitly for convergence toward the U.S. model, a position I find troubling. Rather than harmonizing, then, it may be better to think in terms of raising minimum standards in various areas such as disclosure while allowing nations to exceed them.

Fukao could more fully discuss the systemic evolution that is occurring in such countries as the United States and Japan. In Japan there are some modest pressures to sell stable shareholdings. However, among the most significant changes is the diminished role of lead banks as effective monitors of companies as these companies' reliance on debt capital has fallen. The lack of effective monitoring will accentuate existing weaknesses of the Japanese system. The United States is also changing as the roles of boards of directors are strengthening, institutional investors are becoming more active, and efforts are growing to curb excessive executive compensation. The author needs to offer a fuller set of predictions about the likely extent and significance of these changes if a convincing case is to be made about the need for harmonization in the first place.

Closely related to changes under way is that the U.S. system is being exported to other advanced economies in a variety of ways, perhaps not surprisingly, given the sheer size of the U.S. economy. One route is through U.S. influence on policy thinking in other countries, an influence the United States has traditionally held. For example, the 1986 elimination of capital gains incentives by the United States in the name of "equalizing" the tax treatment of all sources of income has spread to the United Kingdom and other countries. Yet this has actually accentuated the bias against equity investment that exists in the United States and elsewhere because of the double taxation of dividends and retained earnings. U.S. shareholders' increasing investment in foreign equities is also leading to pressures for other countries to conform to American accounting standards, which are (understandably, given the U.S. system) oriented toward providing a fair representation of current earnings. Other forces are also tending to push Japan and Germany toward the U.S. system, some of which Fukao mentions. But he must tackle the likely outcome of this process and whether it will be a desirable one.

Although it would not be optimal for countries to have the same capital allocation system, Fukao's call for a portfolio of systems in each country may beg the question. It does seem sensible to consider whether some of the weaknesses of each country's dominant system could be mitigated through some forms of harmonization. Although the author hints at this, I suspect that this line of thinking could be significantly extended. For example, if a major weakness of the Japanese system is the lack of monitoring by shareholders, it may well be a good thing to harmonize fiduciary responsibilities of financial institutions more toward the American system. Similarly, extending Japanese-style incentives for long-term equity holding to the United States might offset some of the separations between principals and agents that lead to rapid trading. My aim here is not to be exhaustive, but simply to urge a more detailed inquiry into the potential of harmonization to improve the capital allocation systems in individual countries while preserving their differences.

Appendix

Comparison of Corporate Governance Structures

*T*HIS appendix provides brief but detailed comparisons of aspects of corporate governance structures in the United States, Japan, Germany, France and the United Kingdom. In addition to the works cited in chapter 2, it relies on the following sources.

Accounting Rules: Nobes and Parker (1991), Fédération des Experts Comptables Européens (1993), and Tzamouranis and others (1993).

Bankrupcy codes: Carr (1990), Frankel and Montgomery (1991), Japan Center for International Finance (1991), and Franks and Torons (1992).

European Union: Franks and Mayer (1990), Lomas (1990), and Mazur and van Leeuwen (1990).

France: Charbit (1990) and Le Gall and Morel (1992).

Germany: Aizawa (1989), Schmalenbach (1990), *Jura Europae Gesellschaftsrecht*, vol. 1 (1990 or 1991), Schneiderlenne (1992), and Kansaku (1994a and 1994b).

Japan: Taniguchi (1987), Namiki (1989), Ishiguro (1990), Kishida (1991), Maeda (1991), and Ueno (1992).

United Kingdom: KPMG Peat Marwick McLintock (1990a, 1990b), Norton Rose M5 Group (1990), Renshall and Walmsley (1990), Simpson (1990), Younghusband and Wilson (1990), and Panel on Takeovers and Mergers (1993).

United States: Namiki (1989), Namiki and Namiki (1989), Heard (1990), Pickens (1990), Easterbrook and Fischel (1991), Jacobs (1991), Diamond and Williams (1993), and Roe (1993).

General Governance Structures

United States

Because the structure of U.S.companies is ruled by state corporate laws rather than federal law, it is difficult to cover all aspects of that structure. However, many of the largest companies are incorporated in Delaware, which often sets the standards for U.S. corporate law. Securities and Exchange Commission rules regulate the capital market at the federal level.

State corporate laws generally allow companies to choose the method of organization they prefer. In many cases directors are elected at a shareholders' meeting by simple majority for one- to three-year terms. (According to a survey by the Investor Responsibility Research Center, 57 percent of 1,500 publicly traded companies have staggered terms of three years; the shareholders elect one-third of the directors each year.[1]) In most U.S. companies the shareholders can remove a director at the annual meeting (with or without cause, depending on the articles of incorporation) by a simple majority. In the past most directors were involved in the management of the company, but as the share of outside directors has increased on the boards of many companies, the role of the board has become one of overseeing the management of the company, which is carried out by a management team headed by chief executive officer (CEO). This management team is chosen by the board of directors.

The board of directors has broad discretion in running a company. The directors can decide on their own compensation, the amount of dividends to be declared, and other business without asking shareholders. Usually, a shareholders' meeting cannot make binding resolutions on matters of ordinary business, including these matters. Courts recognize the "business judgment rule" and do not hold management liable for bad business decisions, except for cases of gross negligence.

The code of conduct for directors regarding conflict of interest is strict. Especially if a director of a company is involved with a

---

1. Jacobs (1991, p. 80).

second company (as a director, for instance), transactions with the second company are voidable unless they are fair to the first company.

The limited liability of shareholders is sometimes denied for major corporate shareholders of companies with insufficient capitalization facing unpaid employee compensation, trade credits, or tort liabilities.

Japan

Directors are elected at a shareholders' meeting by a simple majority. The term of a director, no more than two years, is set by the articles of incorporation (most companies adopt two-year terms). By a two-thirds majority, shareholders can dismiss a director with or without cause (in the latter case, with compensation). The board of directors elects one or more of its members to represent the company in its dealings with third parties. One of the representative directors is named president (*shacho*) and is usually the most powerful person in the company. Most directors of Japanese companies are promoted from among senior employees and are executive directors.

The shareholders' meeting can vote only on the matters stipulated by the corporate law or the articles of incorporation. However, by amending the articles of incorporation with a two-thirds majority, a shareholders' meeting can vote on other matters, including ordinary business. Total compensation for directors and the amount of dividends must be approved by a shareholders' meeting.

Japanese courts have traditionally not interpreted the business judgment rule as broadly as U.S. courts, but recent lower court rulings have interpreted the rule more broadly. Directors are liable for the damage caused to the company by conflict of interest. Normal transactions among corporations that have directors in common are not automatically deemed conflict-of-interest transactions.

Courts rarely deny the limited liability of shareholders of large companies.

Germany

Relatively few stock corporations (AGs) have publicly traded stock (665 in 1991 out of some 3,000). Most companies—more than 350,000—adopt limited liability company structures (GmbH). This is partly because there is a regulation that requires AGs to have powerful supervisory boards with the participation of employees. Although all AGs are required to have supervisory boards, GmbHs with fewer than 500 employees are not required to do so. The employees have half the seats on the supervisory boards of AGs or GmbHs with more than 2,000 employees. In those AGs with fewer than 2,000 and GmbHs with fewer than 2,000 but more than 500 employees, a third of the supervisory board members must be employee representatives.

The shareholders' meeting elects shareholder representatives to the supervisory board for a maximum of four years. The employees elect their representatives to the supervisory board. In principle, the supervisory board elects a chairman and a deputy by a two-thirds majority from among its members. If this is not possible, the shareholder representatives elect the chairman and the employee representatives elect the deputy. Because the chairman has the tiebreaking vote in the event of deadlock, shareholder representatives have the upper hand on the supervisory board. The shareholders' meeting may remove a shareholder representative with a three-fourths majority vote. Employees may remove their representatives with the same majority. The supervisory board supervises the board of managing directors, which runs the company. No one can be a member of both the board of managing directors and the supervisory board of the same company. The supervisory board meets two to four times a year and depends on information from the board of managing directors.

The board of managing directors of AGs, members of which are elected by the supervisory board, is appointed for a fixed term of up to five years. Most members are appointed for five-year terms. The members can only be removed for good cause, such as a clear breach of duty by the supervisory board. The managing board must take into account the interest of the employees and the public as well as that of the shareholders.

Compensation of the members of the supervisory board is determined by the shareholders' meeting. Compensation of the members of the managing board is decided by the supervisory board. The compensation must be reasonable and in line with the financial situation of the company. The articles of incorporation can be amended with a three-quarters majority vote of a shareholders' meeting.

France

French corporate law provides for two forms of limited liability companies: SA (société anonyme), which is suitable for large firms, and SARL (société à responsabilité limitée), which is for small firms with a maximum of fifty shareholders. SAs can be organized in either of two forms: a corporation managed by a board of directors (the traditional management structure) or a corporation managed by an executive board and a supervisory board, a form inspired by the German system and introduced in 1966. Most corporations are managed by a board of directors.

The directors of traditional SAs are appointed at a shareholders' meeting after being proposed by the board of directors. The meeting is free to dismiss any director through a resolution adopted by a simple majority and to appoint a new director even if the dismissal action has not been put on the agenda. The term of a director is set by the articles of incorporation and is for no more than six years. The total compensation is set at the annual shareholders' meeting. In companies with fifty or more employees, representatives of a workers' committee are entitled to attend all meetings of the board of directors in an advisory capacity. The chairman of the board and the executive officers (the officers need not be directors) are appointed by the board and are responsible for the management of the company. The board of directors determines the remuneration of the chairman and the executive officers, who represent the corporation in relations with third parties. In traditional SAs, the role of the board of directors is often limited to one of control; actual management is carried out by the chairman of the board and the executive officers.

In the new German-style structure, the executive board manages the corporation and the supervisory board supervises the action of the executive board without otherwise taking part in the conduct of the corporation's affairs. The members of the supervisory board are appointed by a shareholders' meeting. The term is set by the articles of incorporation for six years or less. Board members may be dismissed at any time at a shareholders' meeting with a resolution supported by a simple majority. Board members' compensation is decided by a shareholders' meeting. No one can be a member of both the executive board and the supervisory board of the same company. Representatives of a workers' committee are entitled to attend all meetings of the supervisory board in an advisory capacity. The supervisory board appoints the members of the executive board, which carries out general management duties. The term of a member of the executive board is four years, and members may be removed only by a resolution of a shareholders' meeting on the proposal of the supervisory board. As a result, the members of the executive board are better protected than are the chairman and the executive officers of traditional SAs. Their individual compensation is decided by the supervisory board.

In both forms of SAs, a two-thirds majority vote of an extraordinary shareholders' meeting is required to alter the articles of incorporation. Courts may decide to nullify a decision of a board of directors or a shareholders' meeting when there is evidence that the decision was detrimental to the interest of the corporation or to the minority or the majority shareholders' interest and was dictated only by the self-interest of certain shareholders. For instance, the courts could become involved if a board of directors refused for many years to distribute dividends without investing in the expansion of the operations or if a board paid excessive compensation to senior management. The total compensation paid to the five or ten highest-paid employees has to be disclosed to all shareholders.

The statutory auditors are strongly independent of the management and have authority to review the operation of SAs.

United Kingdom

There are two types of limited liability companies in the United Kingdom: public and private. Public companies can offer shares and debentures to the public but also face stricter regulations than do private companies. Directors are elected by a shareholders' meeting with a simple majority vote (however, twenty-seven of Britain's top fifty-two companies have adopted provisions by which all or some of their executive directors need never seek reelection by shareholders).[2] Usually one-third of the directors must retire each year, though the articles of association can provide otherwise. A shareholders' meeting can remove a director before the end of his term with a simple majority vote. Directors are often employees, that is, they are executive directors. Power to appoint additional directors is frequently conferred on the directors by the articles. Casual vacancies are normally filled by nominations from the directors. The directors act by majority vote, and the chairman normally has a tiebreaking vote. Shareholders are not entitled to dividends until the directors allow them. To alter the articles of association, a three-quarter majority of the votes of a shareholders' meeting is required.

The articles of association usually stipulate that the remuneration of the directors be determined at a shareholders' meeting. A director may hold salaried employment in the company under an employment contract. The salary under this employment contract can be decided by the board of directors. Companies are required to disclose the aggregate amounts of directors' compensation (including salaries of employment contracts) in the notes to their accounts.

Traditionally, articles of association have placed restrictions on the borrowing power of directors, often based on a multiple (generally 1.5 to 2.0 times) of share capital and reserves shown in the latest audited accounts. Usually an ordinary resolution is required to raise this limit.

2. Sheridan and Kendall (1992, p. 85).

Transferability of Shares

United States

The charter of a U.S. corporation can put reasonable restrictions on the transfer of shares, but such restrictions are usually seen only in closely held companies. The board of directors sometimes restricts the transfer of shares in the event of takeover offers by invoking a so-called poison pill defense.

Japan

In principle, shares in Japanese companies are fully transferable. A corporation may, however, require in its charter that shareholders obtain the consent of the board of directors to transfer shares. In this case a shareholder may request the company to designate a buyer. This restriction is most often seen in closely held companies.

Germany

The articles of incorporation of German companies may require shareholders to obtain the consent of the company (usually the board of directors) to transfer registered shares. There is no barrier to the transfer of bearer shares in an AG, and most shares are bearer shares.

France

There is no barrier to the transfer of bearer shares in France, and most shares are bearer shares. However, listed companies may in the articles of association limit transferability of registered shares. Transferability may also be limited by establishing private companies that hold the equity of a group of shareholders.

United Kingdom

Listed companies may limit transferability of shares in their articles of incorporation, but the U.K. Stock Exchange requires that the articles should not restrict the transfer of fully paid shares.

Voting rights of Shareholders

United States

A U.S.corporation can issue shares with different voting rights, but few publicly traded companies have multiple classes of common stocks with different voting rights. It is usual to issue preferred shares with priority in receiving dividends but that have limited voting rights. Some companies have amended their charters to require shareholder approval with a super majority (as much as 90 percent) for transactions involving a change of control.

Japan

Japanese corporations are forbidden to issue shares with different voting rights, except for preferred shares. The number of shares without votes cannot exceed one-third of those outstanding. Preferred shares have rarely been issued by Japanese companies: interest payments on debt can be deducted from taxable income, but dividends have to be paid from after-tax income.

Germany

AGs can issue nonvoting preferred shares up to an amount equal to that of all voting shares issued. A company can limit the voting power of an individual shareholder to a certain amount (5 to 10 percent) of the company's shares by amending its articles of incorporation through a three-quarters majority vote of a shareholders' meeting. A company can also limit the voting power of a shareholder through use of a graduated scale by amending its articles. Various large German companies, including Mannesmann (5 percent), Deutsche Bank (5 percent), and BASF and Bayer (5 percent), have this limit on voting rights.

France

People who have held shares in a company for a specified period (perhaps two to four years) may be entitled by the articles of incorporation to double votes. Such clauses can be inserted in the articles by the decision (a two-thirds majority) of an extraordinary meeting of shareholders. The articles may limit the maximum number of votes any shareholders may cast, provided that the limitation applies equally to all shareholders. Up to 25 percent of capital may be issued as investment certificates that can only be transferred to other holders of investment certificates.

United Kingdom

The U.K. Stock Exchange has discouraged the use of discriminatory voting rights as a means of limiting transfers of control, although some differential voting shares are listed. Less than 1 percent of corporations have dual-class shares.

Shareholder Proposal Process

United States

Any shareholder who has at least $1,000 (or 1 percent, whichever is less) of a company's stock for more than one year can put a proposal on a proxy at the company's expense. A vote on a shareholder proposal is nonbinding on management. Shareholders cannot offer their own candidate for director seats through this process. If they wish to challenge management's nominees for directors, they must finance their own proxy campaigns, the cost of which can be very high.

Until November 1992, SEC rules stipulated that all communications among more than ten shareholders on proxy issues first had to be reviewed and approved by the SEC. Since then any shareholder has been allowed to communicate with an unlimited number of other shareholders, provided the shareholder owns less than 5 percent of the shares, has no special interest in the issue being discussed, and is not seeking proxy authority.

Japan

Any shareholder who has at least 300 shares (or 1 percent, whichever is less) of a company's stock for more than six months can put a proposal on a proxy at the company's expense. A vote on a shareholder proposal is binding on management. Shareholders can offer their own candidates for directors' seats through this process.

Any shareholder who has at least 3 percent of a company's stock for more than six months may request that the company hold a shareholders' meeting by indicating the reason for it and the agenda. If the company does not convene a meeting without delay, the shareholder can convene a meeting with court approval and can request the company to pay reasonable expenses of the meeting.

Germany

Any shareholder (no minimum number of shares is required) may request a German company to notify other shareholders of a resolution proposed by him and relating to an item on the agenda of a general meeting. He may also offer his own candidate for the supervisory board and request that all shareholders be notified. But for a resolution on an item not on the agenda, only shareholders who together hold 5 percent of the capital, or shares with an aggregate nominal value of DM 1 million, may request company notification of other shareholders.

France

Any shareholders holding the following minimum amount of shares of a French corporation may require resolutions drafted by them to be put on the agenda of a meeting.

Total corporate capital	Minimum amount of shares
Less than Fr 5 million	5 percent
Fr 5 million to Fr 50 million	2.5 percent of capital between Fr 5 million and Fr 50 million plus Fr 200,000
Fr 50 million to Fr 100 million	1 percent of capital between Fr 50 million and Fr 100 million plus Fr 1,325,000
More than Fr 100 million	0.5 percent capital in excess of Fr 100 million plus Fr 1,825,000

United Kingdom

Any shareholders holding no less than 5 percent of a British company's voting shares or no fewer than 100 shareholders of the company (on average holding more than £100), can propose resolutions for the annual shareholders' meeting. The proposing shareholders have to pay the expense of circulating the resolution. Any shareholder who has at least 10 percent of the company's shares can request the company to convene an extraordinary general meeting by stating the object of the meeting to be called. Often it is difficult to know the names of true shareholders because of the system of nominee shareholdings.

Communications among shareholders are restricted by the Financial Service Act of 1986. All written communications to other shareholders must either be made by an authorized person (under the FSA) or be approved by such a person.

Regulations on Bank Shareholdings in Nonfinancial Companies

United States

U.S. banks cannot hold shares of other large companies. Bank holding companies, however, are allowed to hold up to 5 percent of a company's voting shares and up to 25 percent of total shareholders' equity.

Japan

Japanese financial institutions (including banks) cannot hold or purchase more than 5 percent (10 percent for insurance companies) of the issued shares of Japanese companies without approval from the Fair Trade Commission. The limit was effectively 10 percent until 1987 because of the ten-year grace period allowed under the more restrictive regulations adopted in 1977.

Germany

There is no limit on the share of a nonfinancial company's capital that can be invested by German banks. However, a bank's investment in real estate (buildings, land, and so forth), together with its holdings in other banks and in industrial companies, may not exceed the bank's own capital.

Banks exercise power through the voting rights associated with their custody of the bearer shares of private investors. Although they must follow their shareholders' instructions, banks also notify the shareholders of how they propose to vote at a shareholders' meeting if the shareholders do not give instructions. As a result, major banks can exercise more than 50 percent of the total votes of a number of large AGs. Banks often sit on the supervisory boards of AGs, and in some cases a bank's representative is chairman of the board.

France

There is no limit on a French bank's shareholdings in other companies in terms of the share of the companies' capital. However, there is a limit on bank shareholding in individual corporations in terms of the size of the bank's capital.

United Kingdom

Banks can hold shares of other companies after a review by the Bank of England.

European Union

Under the second European Community banking directive, no single participation in nonfinancial companies may exceed 15 percent of a bank's capital, and a bank's total industrial holdings may not exceed 60 percent of equity capital.

Rules and Practice of Acquisitions

United States

There were more than one hundred tender offers a year in the United States in the second half of the 1980s. To start a tender offer to buy more than 5 percent of a company's shares, a potential acquirer must submit a statement to the SEC. This statement identifies the acquirer, the planned amount of the purchase, the source of financing, and the purpose of the acquisition. Shareholders who acquire more than 5 percent of a corporation must submit a similar statement to the SEC within ten days of acquisition. The management of the target corporation of a tender offer is required to express its opinion on the offer to its shareholders within ten days after the start of the bid. When this opinion is negative, the tender offer is often called a hostile takeover attempt. It is possible to eliminate small shareholders by forcibly buying their shares with cash or other assets (so-called cash-out mergers).

Japan

Most mergers and acquisitions in Japan are carried out as friendly actions proposed by the boards of directors to the shareholders and approved by them. The shares of the disappearing company are usually exchanged with those of the remaining one. Hostile takeovers are very rare. There were only three public tender offers between the adoption of a tender-offer rule in 1971 and the latest change in 1990, and all were friendly. Most past hostile attempts to acquire large blocks of shares were green mailings, and their opaque transactions had been criticized by many observers.

In 1990 major revisions of the rules of public tender offers increased transparency in the market. It is now necessary to conduct a public tender offer to increase holdings beyond 33 percent of a company's shares. To start a tender offer, a potential acquirer must announce it in at least two newspapers and submit a statement disclosing the details of the offer to the minister of finance on the day of the announcement. (Until 1990 it was necessary to submit a statement to the minister of finance at least ten days before the start of a tender offer, which made starting an offer difficult.) There is no threshold above which it becomes compulsory for a buyer to make a public offer for all the company's shares. The management of the target company of a tender offer is not required to express its opinion on the offer to its shareholders, but if it does express an opinion, it has to notify the minister of finance of the statement.

A shareholder who holds 5 percent of the shares of a company has to submit a statement to the minister of finance within five days of the acquisition of more shares. He also has to submit a similar statement when his holding changes more than 1 percent.

Germany

Most acquisitions of German companies are purchases of a majority of shares. Full acquisitions are rare. Until recently, hostile takeovers were very rare.

Under the Securities Exchange Law of July 1994, a purchaser has to notify the target company and the newly created Federal Securities and Exchange Agency as soon as specified percentages of the share ownership are reached, exceeded, or undercut. These percentages are 5, 10, 25, 50, and 75 percent. Before the legislation a purchaser had to disclose the acquisition of more than 25 and 50 percent of outstanding shares. There is no threshold at which it becomes compulsory for a buyer to make a public offer for all a company's shares.

France

Hostile takeovers, which were rare in France until recently, are increasing. It is difficult to take over large French firms because banks, insurance companies, or the government often hold controlling shares. If a buyer acquires more than 33 percent of the target shares, it is obliged to start a full takeover (until March 1992, bidding for only two-thirds of shares was required). The board of directors must express its opinion on an attempted tender offer. The government has often intervened in takeover attempts.

United Kingdom

A number of hostile takeovers have involved large companies. Under the City Code on Takeovers and Mergers, any buyer who acquires more than 30 percent of a target firm (taken together with shares held by shareholders acting in concert with the buyer) is required to make a full takeover bid. Similarly, any shareholder with 30 to 50 percent of the shares with voting rights (together with persons acting in concert with him) has to make a full takeover bid when he acquires more than 2 percent more of the company's shares within a twelve-month period. When 90 percent of the shareholders other than the acquirer accept the tender offer, the acquirer can compulsorily obtain the remaining shares. The board of directors has to express its opinion on an attempted tender offer.

The acquirer of more than 3 percent of a target company's shares has to notify the company within two business days. The company in turn must disclose the names of large shareholders within three business days.

European Union

As part of the single European market, the European Union will require minimum standards for public disclosure rules. According to EC directive 88/627 on participation of listed companies, a purchaser has to notify the target company and the relevant authorities as soon as certain percentages of the target are reached, exceeded, or undercut. These steps are 10, 20, 33 1/3 (in place of 20 and 33 1/3, 25 can be used), 50, and 66 2/3 (or 75) percent. The implementation date for all member states was January 1991.

A proposal in January 1989 for a thirteenth council directive on corporate law concerning takeovers provides that any buyer wanting to acquire shares above a certain threshold (to be fixed by the member states at no more than 33 1/3 percent) shall be obliged to make a full takeover bid.

Countermeasures against Takeover Threats

United States

A number of measures are available to U.S. firms to counter takeover threats.[3]

---

3. Roe (1993); and Weston and others (1990).

—Antitakeover amendments (shark repellents). Various amendments of a corporate charter, which must be approved by shareholders, can make takeover difficult. A super-majority amendment requires shareholder approval of a sale by at least a two-thirds majority and as much as a 90 percent majority for all transactions involving change of control. A fair-price amendment is a super-majority amendment with an additional clause waiving the super-majority requirement if a fair price (commonly defined as the highest price paid by the bidder during a specified period) is paid for all purchased shares. A final tactical amendment may prohibit shareholders from calling a shareholders' meeting.

—Share repurchase. Share repurchases, especially with a premium over the market price, signal that the management thinks that a company's shares are undervalued. By paying out liquid assets the management can also discourage raiders who are planning to repay borrowed funds by selling the assets of the firm.

—Golden parachute. In the event of a hostile takeover attempt, the managers of a target firm may be eligible for large severance payments. This tactic may increase the cost of the takeover somewhat, but it can also weaken management's resistance to a takeover.

—Poison pill. To issue to shareholders securities such as options that are exercisable only after a triggering event such as a tender offer is to confront potential buyers with a poison pill. The securities are designed to make the cost of acquisition very expensive unless the board of directors of the target company consents to the takeover.

—Leveraged recapitalization. In a leveraged recapitalization, outside shareholders (those not involved in the management of the firm) receive a large one-time dividend, while inside shareholders such as directors receive new shares of stock. The cash dividend is mostly financed with borrowed funds. This reorganization will increase the leverage of the corporation by placing ownership of more shares in the hands of management.

—Changes in state law. In the second half of the 1980s, many states introduced changes in state law that restricted hostile takeovers. The changes are in some respects similar to the antitakeover amendments to corporate charters. For example, some statutes require potential buyers to file their intentions with the state, require them to wait before commencing an offer, and sometimes allow the state administrator to determine the fairness of the offer and stop it if it is unfair. Stronger laws deny voting rights to control shares: once an acquirer reaches a specified percentage of target shares—20, 33, or 50 percent—he cannot vote. Some statutes require that other shareholders vote to approve the voting rights of the control shareholders. More recent laws validate poison pills and expand the corporate constituency to allow directors to consider—or mandate that they consider—the effect of a takeover on employees, communities, suppliers, and customers. Most states now have such constituency-expanding statutes. Other laws restrict mergers between a target and an interested shareholder, usually defined as any shareholder owning more than 10 or 15 percent of the target's stock.[4]

Japan

A board of directors of a Japanese company can issue new shares and privately place them with friendly holders to stabilize the share ownership. Until 1966, private placements required shareholders' approval, but the requirement was eliminated for those shares offered at close to market prices. This procedure has often been used to strengthen cross-shareholdings.

Because of the high percentages of stable shareholders, a hostile takeover is extremely difficult to conclude successfully. Otherwise, many of the defensive measures available to U.S. firms are not available to those in Japan. Golden parachutes require shareholders' approval; poison pills are likely to be illegal under Japanese commercial codes; leveraged recapitalization will be difficult, given strict limitations on dividend payouts; and share repurchase is generally prohibited.

Germany

A hostile takeover is very difficult to conclude in Germany because of various institutional factors. Seventy-five percent of shareholders' votes are required to dismiss members of the super-

4. Roe (1993, pp. 338–40).

visory board elected by shareholders. One-third to one-half of the supervisory board members are representatives of the employees. It is not possible to dismiss managing directors during their term without cause. AGs can also limit the voting power of an individual shareholder irrespective of the percentage of shares held by amending the articles of incorporation. This restriction is not applicable to proxy votes held by banks.

France

French target companies have recourse to a court order that grants double voting rights to owners of shares paid up for the previous two to four years. The articles of incorporation may also limit the maximum number of votes any shareholder may cast, provided that the limitation applies equally to all shareholders.

Regulations on Interlocking Shareholdings

United States

U.S. antitrust laws prohibit the acquisition by one company of the shares of another if adverse effects on competition are likely to result. The relatively strict standard of conduct for directors regarding conflict of interest may prevent the development of interlocking shareholding among firms with long-term relationships.

Japan

Japanese antitrust law forbids the establishment of holding companies. Majority-owned subsidiaries may not hold shares in their parent companies. And when a company holds more than 25 percent of the shares of another company, the shares of the former company held by the latter lose votes. Antitrust law also prohibits the acquisition by one company of the shares of another if adverse effects on competition are likely to result. The shareholding of Japanese corporations by large nonfinancial companies (more than ¥10 billion of legal capital or ¥30 billion of net assets) is also limited up to the amount of legal capital or net assets, whichever is larger.

Germany

Majority-owned German subsidiaries are forbidden to hold shares in their parent companies; otherwise reciprocal shareholding is allowed. However, when each company owns more than 25 percent of the shares of the other company, their voting rights are limited to 25 percent irrespective of the size of their holdings.

France

A company may not own shares of another company if the latter holds more than 10 percent of the capital of the former. A subsidiary of a corporation can hold up to 10 percent of the shares of its parent. However, voting rights attached to such shares are not taken into account at the parent company's shareholders' meetings.

United Kingdom

The City Code on Takeovers and Mergers discourages the accumulation of cross-shareholdings as a method of preventing transfers of ownership.

Regulations on Insider Trading

United States

SEC rule 10b-5 prohibits fraud, untrue statements, or omission of important facts in connection with the purchase or sale of any security. Based on this rule, U.S. court decisions generally indicate that directors, officers, and other persons such as lawyers involved with a corporation are forbidden to trade its securities if they have important information regarding the corporation that is not available to the public. In recent years it has often been judged illegal for an outsider to trade on the basis of "misappropriated" information (for example, if an employee of a printing firm were to trade

securities based on customers' information about their companies). The penalty for violating this rule is very severe compared
with that in other countries. The violators have to give back their
illegal profits and have to pay a civil penalty to the U.S. treasury of
up to three times as much as their gains. They also face up to ten
years imprisonment and a $1 million fine.

Security Exchange Act section 16(a) requires a corporation's
insiders (directors, officers, and large shareholders) to report all
their transactions involving its shares to the SEC. Section 16(b)
allows a corporation or its security holders to sue for return of
profits on corporate insiders' transactions that are realized within
a six-month holding period.

Japan

Security Transaction Act article 157 generally prohibits the
employment of deceptive measures (fraud) in security transactions. Infringement of this rule is punishable by up to three years
imprisonment or a ¥3 million fine or both. Although this rule
generally corresponds to SEC rule 10b-5, it has never been applied
to insider trading cases because of its ambiguity. To strengthen the
rule against insider trading, the Security Transaction Act was
amended in 1988, and articles 166 and 167 were added. The
articles prohibit transactions of a company's securities by corporate insiders who have important information about the firm until
the information is publicly disclosed. The penalty for violating
these rules is up to six months imprisonment or a ¥500,000 fine or
both. Directors of a corporation and shareholders who own more
than 10 percent of its shares have to report transactions involving
its shares (including warrants, options, and convertible bonds) to
the minister of finance. The corporation may request them to
return the profit on their transactions realized within a six-month
holding period.

Germany

Until very recently Germany had no explicit legislation against
insider trading, although there were self-policing rules for market

participants. The penalty for violating the rules was the return of the illegal profit. In July 1994 new legislation making insider trading a criminal offence was passed.[5] The law prohibits transactions of a company's securities by its directors, employees, and other related persons who have important price-sensitive information about the company until the information is publicly disclosed. The penalty is up to five years imprisonment or a fine or both. To monitor and deter insider trading, the Federal Securities and Exchange Agency was created by the legislation.

France

Insider trading is prohibited by ordinance 67–853 of September 28, 1967. The definition of insider information is restrictive compared with those of other countries discussed here. The penalty for violations is up to two years imprisonment and Fr10,000,000 fine. The amount of the fine can be increased by up to ten times the profit realized and must at least be equal to the amount of such profit. Regulation COB 90–08 also regulates insider trading.

United Kingdom

The Company Securities (Insider Dealing) Act 1985 prohibits transactions involving a company's securities by its directors, employees, and other related persons who have unpublished price-sensitive information about it. The penalty is up to two years' imprisonment and an unlimited fine. This law is supplemented by the Financial Services Act 1986, the Stock Exchange (Model Code), and The City Code on Takeovers and Mergers.

European Union

EC directive 89/592/EEC was adopted in November 1989 to provide minimum guidelines on the regulation on insider trading to EU member countries. The directive prohibits a company's managers, shareholders, and other persons who have access to important undisclosed information about it from trading its trans-

---

5. "Bundesrat Logjam Broken for Holidays," *Financial Times,* July 9–10, 1994, p. 2.

ferable securities. Each member country may decide the appropriate penalty for violation of this rule. The implementation date for all member states was June 1992.

Accounting Rules and Restrictions on Payments to Shareholders

United States

The legal restrictions on cash payments to shareholders (such as dividends or share repurchases) are very weak in the United States. In most states, companies can pay a dividend when net assets exceed the stated capital. Even when the net assets fall short of the stated capital, companies in many states can still pay a dividend from the profits of the most recent two years (the so-called nimble dividend). Generally, companies do not have to allocate all the paid-in capital (the amount paid in by shareholders, including the premium over the face value of shares) to the stated capital and may keep the remainder as the capital surplus. This capital surplus is then available for future dividends. As a result, it is usually possible for the board of directors to pay out dividends or to buy its own shares by reducing its net assets unless the company faces imminent insolvency.

Accounting rules are oriented toward providing economic information to investors (especially shareholders) and less toward the protection of creditors, employees, and other stakeholders. Most marketable securities are evaluated at market prices rather than historical prices. Tax rules have relatively less influence on accounting rules than they do in the other countries discussed here.

Japan

Japanese companies cannot pay dividends or buy back their own shares unless their net worth exceeds the amount of all the paid-in capital. Cash payments to shareholders from the paid-in capital are restricted by law and require the consent of all a company's creditors. Dissenting creditors have to be repaid before payments from the paid-in capital can be made to shareholders. A corporation is also required to retain at least one-tenth of the amount of dividends as a "profit reserve" not available for future dividends until it exceeds one-quarter of the capital. The amount of paid-in premiums that exceeds the face value of shares and the profit reserve may, however, be used by the board of directors (with the consent of shareholders) to offset losses so as to make it easier to resume dividend payments in the future. Unless it has distributable net assets and is explicitly allowed by its articles of incorporation to do so, a corporation may not buy back its own shares.

Most marketable securities are evaluated at historical prices rather than market prices. When market prices fall below historical cost, companies can use market prices to evaluate securities. In the long-run this rule has resulted in measuring the net assets of a company conservatively, given the long-term rising trend of equity prices in Japan.

Tax rules have a strong influence on accounting rules. In recent years accounting rules, especially those regulating disclosure, have been gradually becoming similar to the rules in the United States, which are oriented toward providing economic information to shareholders by evaluating assets at market prices.

Germany

Payment of dividends from paid-in capital is strongly restricted by law. All creditors must be fully repaid or be given satisfactory security before payments from the paid-in capital may be made to shareholders. In addition, AGs are required to retain at least 5 percent of the annual profits as a legal reserve not available for dividends until the reserve reaches one-tenth of the capital. In principle, AGs may not buy back their own shares.

Accounting rules are oriented toward protecting creditors, employees, and other stakeholders by conservatively measuring the net assets of a company and restricting dividend payouts. Marketable securities are usually evaluated at historical prices; market prices are used when prices fall below historical cost. Accounting rules basically require the recognition of all unrealized capital losses and no unrealized capital gains. Tax rules have a strong influence on accounting rules.

France

Payment of dividends from the paid-in capital is strongly restricted by law. All creditors who so request must be fully repaid or be given security before payments from paid-in capital can be made to shareholders. In addition, SAs are required to retain at least 5 percent of the distributable income as a legal reserve not available for future dividends until it reaches one-tenth of the capital.

Accounting rules are oriented toward protecting creditors, employees, and other stakeholders by measuring the net assets of a company conservatively and restricting dividend payouts. Marketable securities are usually evaluated at historical prices; market prices are used when prices fall below historical cost. Tax rules have a strong influence on accounting rules. Consolidated accounts are less influenced by the principle of conservative valuation.

United Kingdom

Legal (common law) restrictions on dividend payments have traditionally been loose. However, the Companies Act 1980 and subsequent amendments now allow companies to distribute only the cumulative excess of realized profits over realized losses. As a result, payment of dividends from paid-in capital is restricted by law. A company may purchase its own shares only out of distributable profits.

Accounting rules are oriented toward providing economic information to investors (especially shareholders) and less toward the protection of other stakeholders, including creditors and employees. Marketable securities are usually evaluated at market prices. Tax rules have relatively less influence on accounting rules than they do in the other European countries or in Japan.

European Union

The fourth directive on company law (adopted in 1978) harmonizes formats and rules of accounting. However, because of a number of options in this directive (for example, the valuation of assets), financial statements of EU companies are still difficult to compare across countries. The seventh directive on company law (adopted in 1983) helped harmonize the scope and method of consolidation, but considerable differences remain.

Bankruptcy Procedures for Corporate Failures

United States

U.S. bankruptcy law contains both liquidation and reorganization (rehabilitation) processes, with a preference for reorganization. The law puts more weight on protecting the debtor than do the laws of other countries. Partly as a result, more than 60,000 corporate bankruptcy proceedings are instituted each year. A debtor can easily obtain an order of relief from creditors without proving insolvency. Under the rehabilitation process (chapter 11 of the bankruptcy code), the management of the failed corporation (called a *debtor in possession*) can usually retain control and has the power of the receiver of an estate. Only the debtor has the right to submit a plan of reorganization during the first 120 days after the start of the process. In chapter 11 there is no obligation of the management or the court to liquidate, even if the liquidation value is greater than the value of the going concern. The contractual order of priority among creditors and shareholders against the assets of the failed corporation is often violated because of the complicated structure of the approval process of the reorganization plan. As a result, the protection of collateral is not very strong: sometimes chapter 11 produces results biased toward managers, shareholders, and junior creditors of a failed corporation at the cost of protecting more senior creditors.

The concept of equitable subordination in U.S. law deters banks from active control of a financially troubled corporate borrower. If a bank is found to exercise effective control over a debtor firm, the court may significantly reduce the priority of the bank's claim relative to the claims of other creditors. The concept of equitable subordination has been increasingly applied in chapter 11 cases.

Japan

Japanese bankruptcy law contains both liquidation and reorganization processes. Because of revisions in the laws, the current system is complicated to apply. Moreover, a formal court procedure for bankruptcy can be costly. Given these factors, private arrangements among creditors and management, often involving banks, are preferred to formal court proceedings. The protection of collateral is strong. However, under one of the reorganization procedures (*kaisha kosei ho*), introduced in 1952 by adopting the American Bankruptcy Act of 1898, chapter 10, protection of collateral is somewhat restricted to facilitate the rehabilitation of a corporation.

Germany

German bankruptcy law contains a liquidation process but no strong reorganization process. Collateral is strongly protected under the law, making it difficult legally to rehabilitate a failed company. As a result, private arrangements among creditors and management, often involving banks, are preferred to formal court proceedings. Major revision of the bankruptcy laws is now under discussion.

France

To protect employment, the bankruptcy law of 1985 strongly emphasizes the rehabilitation of corporations through reorganization rather than their liquidation. Because of this emphasis, the position of creditors is relatively weak compared with that of employees. It is difficult for creditors to have a say in a reorganization plan, which is prepared by an administrator appointed by the commercial court (*tribunal de commerce*), and even secured creditors are often forced to accept large reductions in the value of their claims.

The management of a failed corporation may face strict sanctions. If the tribunal de commerce finds that the negligence of managers (including de facto managers such as parent companies or lending banks) has caused the failure, it may require the managers to make up the shortage in the net assets. Gross mismanagement enables the court to prohibit the managers from managing businesses for at least five years.

United Kingdom

The Insolvency Act of 1986 contains guidelines for both liquidation and reorganization. Even in its strongest rehabilitation process (administration order), the absolute priority rule is generally preserved and creditors are well protected. To avoid unfair bankruptcy procedures, the law establishes nationally certified insolvency practitioners to manage them.

Sanctions against the directors of failed corporations are strict. Courts may impose personal liabilities on a director who has traded wrongfully, that is, failed to take every step to minimize potential loss to the company's creditors after he expected that the company would face insolvent liquidation. This wrongful trading provision may make a financial firm, including a company's bankers, liable as a shadow director, for any actions that contradicted the objective of minimizing the potential loss to all the company's creditors. This possibility discourages banks from participating in informal corporate rescues. Courts have to declare that the directors of a failed corporation are disqualified when their management has been deemed inappropriate. Disqualified directors are not allowed to be involved in the management of corporations for up to fifteen years.

References

Aizawa, Kouetsu. 1989. *Universal Banking*. Nihon Keizai Shinbun-sha (in Japanese).

Ando, Albert, and Alan J. Auerbach. 1991. "The Cost of Capital in Japan: Recent Evidence and Further Results." Paper prepared for the Second Joint Conference on the Recent Changes in the Financial Structure, sponsored by the Ministry of Finance of Japan, FAIR, and Wharton (June).

Aoki, Masahiko. 1990. "Toward an Economic Model of the Japanese Firm." *Journal of Economic Literature* 28 (March): 1–27.

———. 1992. *Nihon Keizai no Sedo Bunseki*. Chikuma Shobo. Translated from Masahiko Aoki, *Information, Incentives, and Bargaining in the Japanese Economy*. 1988. Cambridge University Press.

———. 1994. "The Japanese Firm as a System of Attributes." In *The Japanese Firm: Sources of Competitive Strength*, edited by Masahiko Aoki and Ronald Dore. Oxford University Press.

Asanuma, Banri. 1992. "Japanese Manufacturer-Supplier Relationships in International Perspective: the Automobile Case." In *International Adjustment and the Japanese Firm*, edited by Paul Sheard. Allen & Unwin.

Auerbach, Alan J. 1983. "Taxation, Corporate Financial Policy and the Cost of Capital." *Journal of Economic Literature* 21 (September): 905–40.

Bank of England. 1989. "Corporate Governance and the Market for Companies: Aspects of the Shareholders Role." Discussion Paper 44. London (November).

Bank of Japan. 1994. "The Japanese Employment System." *Bank of Japan Quarterly Bulletin* (May).

Bisignano, Joseph. 1991a. Banking as a Metaphor: Information, Corporate Control and Financial Intermediation." Basle, Switzerland: Bank for International Settlements (May).

———. 1991b. "European Financial Deregulation: the Pressures for Change and the Costs of Achievement." Paper prepared for the Reserve Bank of Australia Conference on Financial Deregulation, Sydney (June 20–21).

Blow, Laura. 1992. "International Differences in the Cost of Capital: A Review of Some Recent Literature." London: Bank of England, Economics Division (January).

Carr, Josephine, ed. 1990. "Solving the Insoluble: A Legal Guide to Insolvency Regulations around the World." *International Financial Law Review*, special supplement (June).

Charbit, Jacques. 1990 "France." In *International Corporate Governance*, edited by Joseph C. F. Lufkin and David Gallagher. Euromoney Book.

Coase, Ronald H. 1972. "Industrial Organization: A Proposal for Research." In *Policy Issues and Research Opportunnities in Industrial Organization*, edited by Victor K. Fuchs, 59-73. National Bureau of Economic Research.

———. 1988. *The Firm, the Market, and the Law.* University of Chicago Press.

Commission of the European Communities. 1992. *Report of the Committee of Independent Experts on Company Taxation.*

Committee on Banking Regulations and Supervisory Practices. 1988. *International Convergence of Capital Measurement and Capital Standards.* Basle, Switzerland: Bank for International Settlements.

Corrigan, Gerald E. 1990. "Financial Structure and Supervision in Germany, Japan, and the United Kingdom." Statement before the Senate Committee on Banking, Housing and Urban Affairs, 101 Cong. 2 sess. (May).

Davis, E. P. 1992. "The Structure, Regulation and Performance of Pension Funds in Nine Industrial Countries." Paper prepared for World Bank project, Income Security for Old Age. Washington.

Demsetz, Harold, and Kenneth Lehn. 1985. "The Structure of Corporate Ownership: Causes and Consequences." *Journal of Political Economy* 93 (December): 1155–76.

Dertouzos, Michael, Richard K. Lester, Robert M. Solow, and the MIT Commission on Industrial Productivity. 1989. *Made in America: Regaining the Productive Edge.* MIT Press.

Diamond, Michael R., and Julie L. Williams. 1993. *How to Incorporate: A Handbook for Entrepreneurs and Professionals,* 2d. ed. John Wiley.

Easterbrook, Frank H., and Daniel R. Fischel. 1991. *The Economic Structure of Corporate Law.* Harvard University Press.

Economic Planning Agency of the Japanese Government. 1992. *Heisei 4 Nendo Nenji Keizai Houkoku.* Tokyo: Okura-sho Insatsu Kyoku.

Federal Office of Trade Information of Germany. 1991. *Doing Business in Germany's New Federal States,* 2d rev. ed.

Fédération des Experts Comptables Européens. 1993. "Comparison of the Prudence and Matching Principles." Discussion Memorandum for OECD Working Group on Accounting Standards. Paris (May).

Fikre, Ted. 1991. "Economic Capsules: Equity Carve-outs in Tokyo." *Federal Reserve Bank of New York Quarterly Review* 15 (Winter): 60–64.

Frankel, Allen B., and John D. Montgomery. 1991. "Financial Structure: An International Perspective." *Brookings Papers on Economic Activity, 1: 257–97.*

Frankel, Jeffrey. 1991. "The Cost of Capital in Japan: A Survey." Pacific Basin Working Paper Series, PB91–5. Federal Reserve Bank of San Francisco (July).

Franks, Julian R., and Colin Mayer. 1990. "Capital Markets and Corporate Control: A Study of France, Germany and the UK." *Economic Policy* 10 (April): 189–231.

———. 1994. "The Ownership and Control of German Corporations." University of Oxford.

Franks, Julian R., and Walter N. Torous. 1992. "Lessons from a Comparison of U.S. and U.K. Insolvency Codes." *Oxford Review of Economic Policy* 8 (Autumn): 70–82.

Freedman, Charles. 1990. "Universal Banking and Integrated Financial Systems: The Canadian View." Unpublished revised notes for presentation to the Seminar on Financial Sector Liberalization, Cambridge, Massachusetts (June).

French, Kenneth R., and James M. Poterba. 1991. "Were Japanese Stock Prices Too High?" *Journal of Financial Economics* 29 (October): 337–63.

Froot, Kenneth A., Andre F. Perold, and Jeremy C. Stein. 1991. "Shareholder Trading Practices and Corporate Investment Horizons." NBER Working Paper 3638. Cambridge, Mass.: National Bureau of Economic Research (March).

Fukao, Mitsuhiro. 1993. "International Integration of Financial Markets and the Cost of Capital." *Journal of International Securities Markets* 7 (Spring-Summer).

Fukao, Mitsuhiro, and Masaharu Hanazaki. 1986. "Internationalization of Financial Markets: Some Implications for Macroeconomic Policy and for the Allocation of Capital." OECD Department of Economics and Statistics Working Papers 37. Paris (November).

———. 1987. "Internationalisation of Financial Markets and the Allocation of Capital." *OECD Economic Studies* 8 (Spring): 35–92.

Hall, Bronwyn H. 1990. "The Impact of Corporate Restructuring on Industrial Research and Development." *Brookings Papers on Economic Activity, Microeconomics* : 85–124.

Heard, James E. 1990. "Institutional Investors and Corporate Governance: The U.S. Perspective." In *International Corporate Governance*, edited by Joseph C. F. Lufkin and David Gallagher. Euromoney Books.

Herring, Richard J., and Robert E. Litan. 1995. *Financial Regulation in a Global Economy.* Brookings.

Hoshi, Takeo, Anil Kashyap, and David Scharfstein. 1990a. "Bank Monitoring and Investment: Evidence from the Changing Structure of Japanese Corporate Banking Relationships." In *Asymmetric Information, Corporate Finance and Investment*, edited by R. Glenn Hubbard, 105–26. University of Chicago Press.

———. 1990b. "The Role of Banks in Reducing the Cost of Financial Distress in Japan." NBER Working Paper 3435. Cambridge, Mass.: National Bureau of Economic Research (September).

Institutional Investor Project. 1991. "Institutional Concentration of Economic Power, A Study of Institutional Holdings and Voting Authority in U.S. Publicly Held Corporations." Columbia University Center for Law and Economic Studies (October).

Ishiguro, Toru. 1990. "Japan." In *International Corporate Governance*, edited by Joseph C. F. Lufkin and David Gallagher. Euromoney Books.

Ito, Kunio. 1991. "M&A in Japan: Some Empirical Results and the Logic of Inter/locking Shareholdings." Paper prepared for the Second Joint Conference on Recent Changes in the Financial Structure, sponsored by the Ministry of Finance of Japan, FAIR, and Wharton (June).

Ito, Motoshige. 1989. "Kigyo kan Kankei to Keizokuteki Torihiki." In *Nihon no Kigyo*, edited by Ken'ichi Imai and Ryutaro Komiya, 109–30. Tokyo University Press.

Jacobs, Michael T. 1991. *Short-Term America: The Causes and Cures of Our Business Myopia*. Harvard Business School Press.

Japan Center for International Finance. 1991. *Shuyo-koku no Tosan Hosei.*

Jenkinson, Tim, and Colin Mayer. 1992. "The Assessment: Corporate Governance and Corporate Control." *Oxford Review of Economic Policy* 8 (Autumn): 1–10.

Jensen, Michael C. 1988. "Takeovers: Their Causes and Consequences." *Journal of Economic Perspectives* 2 (Winter): 21–48.

———. 1991. "Corporate Control and the Politics of Finance." *Journal of Applied Corporate Finance* 4 (Summer): 13–33.

Jensen, Michael C. and Kevin J. Murphy. 1990. "Performance Pay and Top-Management Incentives." *Journal of Political Economy* 4 (April): 225–64.

Jura Europae Gesellschaftsrecht. 1990 or 1991. Vol. 1. Verlag C.H. Beck.

Kagono, Tadao, and Takaoi Kobayashi. 1989. "Shigen Kyoshutsu to Taishutsu Shoheki." In *Nihon no Kigyo*, edited by Ken'ichi Imai and Ryutaro Komiya, 73–92. Tokyo University Press.

Kansaku, Hiroyuki. 1994a. "Doitsu Dainiji Shihon-shijo Shinko Hoan no Gairyaku." *Shoji Homu* 1349 (March 5).

———. 1994b. "Doitsu Dainiji Shihon-shijo Shinko Hoan no Gairyaku." *Shoji Homu* 1349 (April 25).

Kaplan, Steven N. 1993a. "Top Executive Rewards and Firm Performance: A Comparison of Japan and the U.S." Graduate School of Business, University of Chicago (August).

———. 1993b. "Top Executive Turnover and Firm Performance in Germany." Graduate School of Business, University of Chicago (September).

Keizai Kikaku Cho. 1992. *Keizai Hakusho.*

Kester, W. Carl. 1991. *Japanese Takeovers: The Global Contest for Corporate Control.* Harvard Business School Press.

———. 1992. "The Industrial Groups as Systems of Contractual Governance." *Oxford Review of Economic Policy* 8 (Autumn): 24–44.

Kigyo Kodo ni Kansuru Chosa Kenkyu Iinkai. 1988. *Nichi-bei Kigyo Kodo Hikaku Chosa Hokokusho.*

King, M. A., and Don Fullerton, eds. 1984. *The Taxation of Income from Capital: A Comparative Study for the United States, the United Kingdom, Sweden and West Germany.* University of Chicago Press.

Kishida, Masao. 1991. *Zeminaru Kaisha Ho Nyumon.* Nihon Keizai Shinbun-sha.

———. 1994. *Zeminaru Kaisha Ho Nyumon*, 2d ed. Nihon Keizai Shinbun-sha.

Kondo, Mitsuo. 1991. "Kigyo Baishu to Taisho Kaisha (Keieisha) no Taio." *Shoji Homu* 1259 (August): 17–22.

Koshiro, Kazutoshi. 1989. "Koyo Seido to Jinzai Katsuyo Senryaku." In *Nihon no Kigyo,* edited by Ken'ichi Imai and Ryutaro Komiya, 275–317. Tokyo University Press.

KPMG Marwick McLintock. 1990a. *The Companies Acts 1985 and 1989: Accounting and Financial Requirements.* London.

———. 1990b. *Creditors' Meetings: For Insolvency Procedures in England and Wales.* London.

Le Gall, Jean-Pierre, and Paul Morel. 1992. *French Company Law,* 2d ed. Longman.

Lomas, Paul. 1990. "EC ni okeru Insider Torihiki Kisei" *Shoji Homu* 1205 (January): 16–19.

Lufkin, Joseph C. F., and David Gallagher, eds. 1990. *International Corporate Governance.* Euromoney Books.

Maeda, Hitoshi, 1991. *Kaisha Ho Nyumon,* 2d ed. Yubikaku-shoten.

Malkiel, Burton G. 1992. "The Cost of Capital, Institutional Arrangements and Business Fixed Investment: An International Comparison." Paper prepared for the Osaka-Wharton Conference on Corporate Financial Policy and International Competition.

Matsui, Masaru. 1991. "Kaisei Shoken Torihiki Ho ka no Kabushiki Kokai Kaitsuke Tetsuzuki." *Shoji Homu* 1246 (April).

Mattione, Richard. 1992. "A Capital Cost Disadvantage for Japan?" Tokyo: Morgan Guaranty Trust (April).

Mayer, Colin. 1990. "Financial System, Corporate Finance, and Economic Development." In *Asymmetric Information, Corporate Finance and Investment,* edited by Glenn Hubbard, 307–32. University of Chicago Press.

———. 1993. "Ownership." Inaugural lecture to the University of Warwick (February).

Mazur, Anne H., and Gijs C. L. van Leeuwen. 1990. "Corporate Governance in the EEC and Related Matters." In *International Corporate Governance,* edited by Joseph C. F. Lufkin and David Gallagher. Euromoney Books.

McCauley, Robert N., and Steven A. Zimmer. 1989. "Explaining International Differences in the Cost of Capital." *Federal Reserve Bank of New York Quarterly Review* 14 (Summer): 7–28.

———. 1994. "Exchange Rates and International Differences in the Cost of Capital." In *Exchange Rates and Corporate Performance,* edited by Yakov Ahimred and Richard M. Levitch, pp. 119–48. Burr Ridge, Ill.: Irwin Professional Publishing.

Miwa, Yoshiro. 1989. "Shitauke Kankei: Jidosha Sangyo." In *Nihon no Kigyo,* edited by Ken'ichi Imai and Ryutaro Komiya. Tokyo University Press.

Morimoto, Shigeru. "Kigyo Baishu ni kakaru Koi Kisei." *Shoji Homu* 1259 (August): 11–17.

Morita, Akira. 1991. "Kigyo Baishu no Soronteki Kadai." *Shoji Homu* 1259 (August): 4–11.

Namiki, Toshimori. 1989. *Nichi-Bei Insider Torihiki Ho to Kigyo Baishu Ho.* Chuo-keizai-sha.

Namiki, Toshimori, and Kazuo Namiki. 1989. *Gendai Amerika Kaisha Ho.* Chu Keizai sha.

Nihon Keizai Shinbun-Sha. 1990. *Zeminaru Gendai Kigyo Nyumon.*

Nobes, Christopher, and Robert Parker, eds. 1991. *Comparative International Accounting,* 3d ed. Prentice Hall.

Norton Rose M5 Group. 1990. *Mergers and Acquisitions of Public Companies in the United Kingdom.* London.

OECD. 1991. *Taxing Profits in a Global Economy: Domestic and International Issues.* Paris.

———. 1992. *Banks under Stress.* Paris.

Ohba, Tatsuko, and Akiyoshi Horiuchi. 1990. "Hompo-kigyo no Main-Bank Kankei to Setsubi-toshi Kodo no Kankei ni Tsuite." *Kin'yu Kenkyu* 9 (December): 23–50.

———. 1992. "Kigyo no Setsubi Toshi to Main-bank Kankei." *Kin'yu Kenkyu* 11 (March): 37–59.

Panel on Takeovers and Mergers and the Rules Governing Acquisitions of Shares. 1993. *The City Code on Takeovers and Mergers.* London.

Pickens, T. Boone. 1990. "The Shareholders' Proposal Process." In *International Corporate Governance,* edited by Joseph C. F. Lufkin and David Gallagher. Euromoney Books.

Porter, Michael, E. 1992. *Capital Choices: Changing the Way America Invests in Industry.* Washington: Council on Competitiveness.

Prowse, Stephen D. 1990. "Institutional Investment Patterns and Corporate Financial Behavior in the United States and Japan." *Journal of Financial Economics* 27 (September): 43–66.

———. 1992. "The Structure of Corporate Ownership in Japan." *Journal of Finance* 47 (July): 1121–40.

———. 1994. "Corporate Governance in an International Perspective: A Survey of Corporate Control Mechanisms among Large Firms in the United States, the United Kingdom, Japan and Germany." BIS Economic Papers 41. Basle, Switzerland: Bank for International Settlements.

Renshall, Michael, and Keith Walmsley. 1990. *Butterworths Company Law Guide,* 2d. ed. Butterworths.

Ripert, Georges, and René Roblot. 1991. *Traité de Droit Commercial,* vol. 1, 14th ed. Paris: Librarie Générale de Droit et de Jurisprudence.

Roe, Mark J. 1993. "Takeover Politics." In *The Deal Decade: What Takeovers and Leveraged Buyouts Mean for Corporate Governance,* edited by Margaret M. Blair, 321–53 . Brookings.

Romano, Roberta. 1993. "The Genius of American Corporate Law." Washington: American Enterprise Institute.

Rubin, Paul H. 1990. *Managing Business Transactions.* Free Press.

Sakurai, Kojiro. 1991. *Tainichi Chokusetsu Toshi no Bunseki.* Japan Development Bank Chosa 151.

Schmalenbach, Dirk. 1990. "Federal Republic of Germany." In *International Corporate Governance,* edited by Josephy C. F. Lufkin and David Gallagher. Euromoney Books.

Schneider-Lenne, Ellen R. 1992. "Corporate Control in Germany." *Oxford Review of Economic Policy* 8 (Autumn): 11–23.

Sheard, Paul. 1994. "Main Banks and the Governance of Financial Distress." EDI Working Papers 94 (7). Washington: Economic Development Institute of the World Bank.

Sheridan, Thomas, and Nigel Kendall. 1992. *Corporate Governance: An Action Plan for Profitability and Business Success.* Pitman.

Shleifer, Andrei, and Lawrence H. Summers. 1988. "Breach of Trust in Hostile Takeovers." In *Corporate Takeovers: Causes and Consequences,* edited by Alan J. Auerbach, 33–56. University of Chicago Press.

Simpson, Anne. 1990. "Overview of UK Corporate Governance." In *International Corporate Governance,* edited by Joseh C.F. Lufkin and David Gallagher. Euromoney Books

Stiglitz, Joseph E. 1985. "Credit Markets and the Control of Capital." *Journal of Money, Credit and Banking* 17 (May): 133–52.

Szewczyk, Samuel H., and George P. Tsetsekos. 1992. "State Intervention in the Market for Corporate Control: The Case of Pennsylvania Senate Bill 1310." *Journal of Financial Economics* 31 (February): 3–23.

Tachibana, Mitsunobu. 1991. "Kokai Kaituke Seido ni kakaru Sei-Shorei no Kaisetsu." *Shoji Homu* 1238 (January 5):61–64; 1241 (February 15): 23–26; and 1242 (February 25): 27–30.

Taniguchi, Yasuhei, ed. 1987. *Gendai Tosan Ho Nyumon.* Horitu Bunka Sha.

Tzamouranis, Marina, and others. 1993. "European Accounting: Bridging the GAAP." *Journal of International Securities Markets* 7 (Spring-Summer).

Ueno, Hisanori. 1992. *Shin Tosan Shori to Hoteki Giho.* Shoji Homu Kenkyu Kai.

Weston, J. Fred, Kwang S. Chung, and Susan E. Hoag. 1990. *Mergers, Restructuring, and Corporate Control.* Prentice-Hall.

Williamson, Oliver E. 1985. *The Economic Institutions of Capitalism.* Free Press.

Womack, James P., Daniel T. Jones, and Daniel Roos. 1990. *The Machine That Changed the World.* Macmillan Press.

Younghusband, Victoria, and Ian Wilson. 1990. "United Kingdom." In *International Corporate Governance,* edited by Joseph C. F. Lufkin and David Gallagher. Euromoney Books.

Index

133